TAKING BACK
YOUR FAITH
FROM THE
AMERICAN DREAM

RADICAL

DAVID PLATT

MULTNOMAH
BOOKS

RADICAL
PUBLISHED BY MULTNOMAH BOOKS
12265 Oracle Boulevard, Suite 200
Colorado Springs, Colorado 80921

All Scripture quotations, unless otherwise indicated, are taken from the Holy Bible, New International Version®. NIV®. Copyright © 1973, 1978, 1984 by International Bible Society. Used by permission of Zondervan Publishing House. All rights reserved. Scripture quotations marked (KJV) are taken from the King James Version.

Italics in Scripture quotations indicate the author's added emphasis.

Details in some anecdotes and stories have been changed to protect the identities of the persons involved.

ISBN 978-1-60142-568-3
ISBN 978-1-60142-222-4 (electronic)

Copyright © 2010 by David Platt

Published in association with Yates & Yates, LLP, Attorneys and Counselors, Orange, California.

The author's royalties from this book will go toward promoting the glory of Christ in all nations.

Published in the United States by WaterBrook Multnomah, an imprint of the Crown Publishing Group, a division of Random House Inc., New York.

MULTNOMAH and its mountain colophon are registered trademarks of Random House Inc.

The Library of Congress cataloged the original edition as follows:
Platt, David.
    Radical : taking back your faith from the American dream / David Platt. — 1st ed.
        p. cm.
    Includes bibliographical references (p.   ).
    ISBN 978-1-60142-221-7 — ISBN 978-1-60142-222-4 (electronic)
    1. Christian life—United States. 2. Christianity and culture—United States. 3. American Dream—Religious aspects—Christianity. I. Title.
    BV4501.3.P63 2010
    261'.10973—dc22

                                2009046887

Printed in the United States of America
2013

10 9 8 7 6 5 4 3 2 1

Response to *Radical* and *Radical Together*

"I love this book! Please read it. God is using David Platt to lead his church into much-needed reform. *Radical Together* is filled with tremendous insight from a man who loves Christ's church. I don't know of a church leader that I trust more."

—FRANCIS CHAN, best-selling author of *Crazy Love*

"I have the privilege of knowing David Platt, and I assure you that his life and ministry commend what he has written here. Read *Radical Together*. Like the right medicine, it may be more helpful than comfortable. In fact, my prayer is that it may be an explosion, shifting many churches from centering wrongly on ourselves to centering rightly on Christ and his agenda for us—and for his world."

—MARK DEVER, senior pastor, Capitol Hill Baptist Church

"*Radical* caused many Christians to be shaken and to reevaluate their lives. *Radical Together* will do the same for our churches. It is such a clarion call for churches across the world to follow the clear teachings of the Word that I began to pray this book would indeed move thousands of churches to become more biblically radical. Many churches and Christians will never be the same again after reading this book...."

—THOM S. RAINER, president and CEO, LifeWay Christian
Resources, and coauthor of *The Millennials* and *Simple Church*

"David Platt challenges Christians to wake up, trade in false values rooted in the American dream, and embrace the notion that each of us is blessed by God for a global purpose—to make Christ's glory known to all nations! *Radical* is a must-read for every believer!"

—WESS STAFFORD, president and CEO, Compassion International

"Platt's arguments…emerge at a postexcess moment, when attitudes toward material life are up for grabs. His book has struck a chord."

—DAVID BROOKS, *The New York Times*

"Platt challenges affluent Christians to rethink devoting vast resources to providing entertaining experiences and lattes for seekers. His call for faithful allocation of resources and an empowered laity will resonate across the Christian spectrum."

—*Publishers Weekly*

"What's significant about Platt's perspective is that it is coming from a solidly conservative voice in the evangelical mainstream."

—JONATHAN MERRITT, *The Huffington Post*

"This book is a challenge for Christians to wake up, trade in their false 'American dreams,' and live a Christ-centered life."

—JAY PERONI, CFP, *Crosswalk.com*

"[Platt is] biblical, straightforward, brutally honest, and writes powerful narrative…as he sets out to discover what Jesus really taught to first century followers."

—MATTHEW ROBBINS, *TheChristianManifesto.com*

"Throughout the book, Platt exposes the indifference of American evangelicals… It was hard for me to put the book down, though I can't say that I enjoyed it. I was convicted. I was uncomfortable…. But mostly I was (and am) challenged. Challenged to live a life that looks more like that of a true follower of Christ."

—JOHN BIRD, *DiscerningReader.com*

To Heather,
my beautiful bride and best friend

CONTENTS

CHAPTER ONE

SOMEONE WORTH LOSING EVERYTHING FOR

WHAT RADICAL ABANDONMENT TO JESUS REALLY MEANS

"The youngest megachurch pastor in history."

While I would dispute that claim, it was nonetheless the label given to me when I went to pastor a large, thriving church in the Deep South—the Church at Brook Hills in Birmingham, Alabama. From the first day I was immersed in strategies for making the church bigger and better. Authors I respect greatly would make statements such as, "Decide how big you want your church to be, and go for it, whether that's five, ten, or twenty thousand members." Soon my name was near the top of the list of pastors of the fastest-growing U.S. churches. There I was…living out the American church dream.

But I found myself becoming uneasy. For one thing, my model

in ministry is a guy who spent the majority of his ministry time with twelve men. A guy who, when he left this earth, had only about 120 people who were actually sticking around and doing what he told them to do. More like a minichurch, really. Jesus Christ—the youngest minichurch pastor in history.

So how was I to reconcile the fact that I was now pastoring thousands of people with the fact that my greatest example in ministry was known for turning away thousands of people? Whenever the crowd got big, he'd say something such as, "Unless you eat the flesh of the Son of Man and drink his blood, you have no life in you."[1] Not exactly the sharpest church-growth tactic. I can almost picture the looks on the disciples' faces. "No, not the drink-my-blood speech! We'll never get on the list of the fastest-growing movements if you keep asking them to eat you."

By the end of that speech, all the crowds had left, and only twelve men remained.[2] Jesus apparently wasn't interested in marketing himself to the masses. His invitations to potential followers were clearly more costly than the crowds were ready to accept, and he seemed to be okay with that. He focused instead on the few who believed him when he said radical things. And through their radical obedience to him, he turned the course of history in a new direction.

Soon I realized I was on a collision course with an American church culture where success is defined by bigger crowds, bigger budgets, and bigger buildings. I was now confronted with a startling reality: Jesus actually spurned the things that my church culture said were most important. So what was I to do? I found myself faced with two big questions.

The first was simple. *Was I going to believe Jesus?* Was I going to embrace Jesus even though he said radical things that drove the crowds away?

The second question was more challenging. *Was I going to obey Jesus?* My biggest fear, even now, is that I will hear Jesus' words and walk away, content to settle for less than radical obedience to him. In other words, my biggest fear is that I will do exactly what most people did when they encountered Jesus in the first century.

That's why I've written this book. I am on a journey. But I am convinced it is not just a journey for pastors. I am convinced these questions are critical for the larger community of faith in our country today. I am convinced that we as Christ followers in American churches have embraced values and ideas that are not only unbiblical but that actually contradict the gospel we claim to believe. And I am convinced we have a choice.

You and I can choose to continue with business as usual in the Christian life and in the church as a whole, enjoying success based on the standards defined by the culture around us. Or we can take an honest look at the Jesus of the Bible and dare to ask what the consequences might be if we really believed him and really obeyed him.

I invite you to join the journey with me. I do not claim to have all the answers. If anything, I have more questions than answers. But if Jesus is who he said he is, and if his promises are as rewarding as the Bible claims they are, then we may discover that satisfaction in our lives and success in the church are not found in what our culture deems most important but in radical abandonment to Jesus.

PUDDLES OF TEARS

Imagine all the blinds closed on the windows of a dimly lit room. Twenty leaders from different churches in the area sat in a circle on the floor with their Bibles open. Some of them had sweat on their foreheads after walking for miles to get there. Others were dirty from the dust in the villages from which they had set out on bikes early that morning.

They had gathered in secret. They had intentionally come to this place at different times throughout the morning so as not to draw attention to the meeting that was occurring. They lived in a country in Asia where it is illegal for them to gather like this. If caught, they could lose their land, their jobs, their families, or their lives.

I listened as they began sharing stories of what God was doing in their churches. One man sat in the corner. He had a strong frame, and he served as the head of security, so to speak. Whenever a knock was heard at the door or a noise was made outside the window, everyone in the room would freeze in tension as this brother would go to make sure everything was okay. As he spoke, his tough appearance soon revealed a tender heart.

"Some of the people in my church have been pulled away by a cult," he said. This particular cult is known for kidnapping believers, taking them to isolated locations, and torturing them. Brothers and sisters having their tongues cut out of their mouths is not uncommon.

As he shared about the dangers his church members were facing, tears welled up in his eyes. "I am hurting," he said, "and

I need God's grace to lead my church through these attacks."

A woman on the other side of the room spoke up next. "Some of the members in my church were recently confronted by government officials." She continued, "They threatened their families, saying that if they did not stop gathering to study the Bible, they were going to lose everything they had." She asked for prayer, saying, "I need to know how to lead my church to follow Christ even when it costs them everything."

As I looked around the room, I saw that everyone was now in tears. The struggles expressed by this brother and sister were not isolated. They all looked at one another and said, "We need to pray." Immediately they went to their knees, and with their faces on the ground, they began to cry out to God. Their prayers were marked less by grandiose theological language and more by heartfelt praise and pleading.

"O God, thank you for loving us."

"O God, we need you."

"Jesus, we give our lives to you and for you."

"Jesus, we trust in you."

They audibly wept before God as one leader after another prayed. After about an hour, the room drew to a silence, and they rose from the floor. Humbled by what I had just been a part of, I saw puddles of tears in a circle around the room.

In the days since then, God has granted me many other opportunities to gather with believers in underground house churches in Asia. Men and women there are risking everything to follow Christ.

Men like Jian, an Asian doctor who left his successful health clinic and now risks his life and the lives of his wife and two kids in order to provide impoverished villages with medical care while secretly training an entire network of house-church leaders.

Women like Lin, who teaches on a university campus where it is illegal to spread the gospel. She meets in secret with college students to talk about the claims of Christ, though she could lose her livelihood for doing so.

Teenagers like Shan and Ling, who have been sent out from house churches in their villages to undergo intensive study and preparation for taking the gospel to parts of Asia where there are no churches.

Ling said to me, "I have told my family that I will likely never come back home. I am going to hard places to make the gospel known, and it is possible that I will lose my life in the process."

Shan added, "But our families understand. Our moms and dads have been in prison for their faith, and they have taught us that Jesus is worthy of all our devotion."

A DIFFERENT SCENE

Three weeks after my third trip to underground house churches in Asia, I began my first Sunday as the pastor of a church in America. The scene was much different. Dimly lit rooms were now replaced by an auditorium with theater-style lights. Instead of traveling for miles by foot or bike to gather for worship, we had arrived in millions of dollars' worth of vehicles. Dressed in our fine clothes, we sat down in our cushioned chairs.

To be honest, there was not much at stake. Many had come

because this was their normal routine. Some had come simply to check out the new pastor. But none had come at the risk of their lives.

That afternoon, crowds filled the parking lot of our sprawling multimillion-dollar church campus. Moms, dads, and their kids jumped on inflatable games. Plans were being discussed for using the adjacent open land to build state-of-the-art recreation fields and facilities to support more events like this.

Please don't misunderstand this scene. It was filled with wonderful, well-meaning, Bible-believing Christians who wanted to welcome me and enjoy one another. People like you and people like me, who simply desire community, who want to be involved in church, and who believe God is important in their lives. But as a new pastor comparing the images around me that day with the pictures still fresh in my mind of brothers and sisters on the other side of the world, I could not help but think that somewhere along the way we had missed what is radical about our faith and replaced it with what is comfortable. We were settling for a Christianity that revolves around catering to ourselves when the central message of Christianity is actually about abandoning ourselves.

TALKING PEOPLE OUT OF FOLLOWING CHRIST

At the end of Luke 9, we find a story about three men who approached Jesus, eager to follow him. In surprising fashion, though, Jesus seems to have tried to talk them out of doing so.

The first guy said, "I will follow you wherever you go."

Jesus responded, "Foxes have holes and birds of the air have nests, but the Son of Man has no place to lay his head."[3] In other words, Jesus told this man that he could expect homelessness on the journey ahead. Followers of Christ are not guaranteed that even their basic need of shelter will be met.

The second man told Jesus that his father had just died. The man wanted to go back, bury his father, and then follow Jesus.

Jesus replied, "Let the dead bury their own dead, but you go and proclaim the kingdom of God."[4]

I remember distinctly the moment when my own dad died unexpectedly of a heart attack. Amid the immense heaviness of the days that followed and the deep desire of my heart to honor my dad at his funeral, I cannot imagine hearing these words from Jesus: "Don't even go to your dad's funeral. There are more important things to do."

A third man approached Jesus and told him that he wanted to follow him, but before he did, he wanted to say good-bye to his family.

Jesus wouldn't let him. He told the man, "No one who puts his hand to the plow and looks back is fit for service in the kingdom of God."[5] Plainly put, a relationship with Jesus requires total, superior, and exclusive devotion.

Become homeless.

Let someone else bury your dad.

Don't even say good-bye to your family.

Is it surprising that, from all we can tell in Luke 9, Jesus was successful in persuading these men not to follow him?

The first time I heard this text preached, it was from the lips of Dr. Jim Shaddix. He was my preaching professor, and I had moved to New Orleans specifically to study under him. Soon after I got there, Dr. Shaddix invited me to travel with him to an event where he was speaking. I sat in the front row in a crowd of hundreds of people, and I listened to his sermon begin.

"Tonight my goal is to talk you out of following Jesus."

My eyebrows shot up in amazement and confusion. What was he thinking? What was *I* thinking? I had just moved my life to New Orleans to study under a guy who persuades people not to follow Jesus.

Dr. Shaddix preached the sermon exactly as Luke 9 describes, giving potential disciples warnings about what is involved in following Jesus. In the end he invited people who wanted to follow Christ to come down to the front. To my surprise many in the crowd got up from their seats and came down. I sat there dumbfounded and began to think, *So this is just a preaching tactic, kind of a sanctified reverse psychology. And it works. Tell them you're going to talk them out of following Jesus, and they will respond in droves.*

I decided I was going to try it.

The next week I was preaching at a youth event. Taking my cue from Dr. Shaddix, I proudly stood before the students assembled that night and announced, "My goal tonight is to talk you out of following Jesus." I could see the leaders of the event raise their eyebrows in concern, but I knew what I was doing. After all, I'd been in seminary a few weeks, and I'd seen this done before. So I preached the message and then invited students who wanted to follow Christ to come forward.

Apparently I was more successful in preaching that message than Dr. Shaddix had been. Let's just say I stood at the front alone for a while until finally the leader who organized the event decided it was time for me to call it a night. For some reason I was never invited back.

Contrary to what I may have thought about Luke 9, Jesus was not using a gimmick to get more followers. He was simply and boldly making it clear from the start that if you follow him, you abandon everything—your needs, your desires, even your family.

RADICAL ABANDONMENT

The events of Luke 9 were not isolated incidents in the life of Jesus, either. On another occasion, when surrounded by a crowd of eager followers, Jesus turned to them and remarked, "If anyone comes to me and does not hate his father and mother, his wife and children, his brothers and sisters—yes, even his own life—he cannot be my disciple."[6] Imagine hearing those words from an obscure Jewish teacher in the first century. He just lost most of us at *hello*.

But then he continued: "Anyone who does not carry his cross and follow me cannot be my disciple."[7] Now this is taking it to another level. *Pick up an instrument of torture and follow me.* This is getting plain weird…and kind of creepy. Imagine a leader coming on the scene today and inviting all who would come after him to pick up an electric chair and become his disciple. Any takers?

As if this were not enough, Jesus finished his seeker-sensitive plea with a pull-at-your-heartstrings conclusion. "Any of you who does not give up everything he has cannot be my disciple."[8] Give up everything you have, carry a cross, and hate your family. This sounds a lot different than "Admit, believe, confess, and pray a prayer after me."

And that's still not all. Consider Mark 10, another time a potential follower showed up. Here was a guy who was young, rich, intelligent, and influential. He was a prime prospect, to say the least. Not only that, but he was eager and ready to go. He came running up to Jesus, bowed at his feet, and said, "What must I do to inherit eternal life?"[9]

If we were in Jesus' shoes, we probably would be thinking this is our chance. A simple "Pray this prayer, sign this card, bow your head, and repeat after me," and this guy is in. Then think about what a guy like this with all his influence and prestige can do. We can get him on the circuit. He can start sharing his testimony, signing books, raising money for the cause. This one is a no-brainer—we have to get him in.

Unfortunately, Jesus didn't have the personal evangelism books we have today that tell us how to draw the net and close the sale. Instead Jesus told him one thing: "Go, sell everything you have and give to the poor, and you will have treasure in heaven. Then come, follow me."[10]

What was he thinking? Jesus had committed the classic blunder of letting the big fish get away. The cost was too high.

Yet the kind of abandonment Jesus asked of the rich young man is at the core of Jesus' invitation throughout the Gospels. Even his simple call in Matthew 4 to his disciples—"Follow me"—contained radical implications for their lives. Jesus was calling them to abandon their comforts, all that was familiar to them and natural for them.

He was calling them to abandon their careers. They were reorienting their entire life's work around discipleship to Jesus. Their plans and dreams were now being swallowed up in his.

Jesus was calling them to abandon their possessions. "Drop your nets and your trades as successful fishermen," he was saying in effect.

Jesus was calling them to abandon their family and their friends. When James and John left their father, we see Jesus' words in Luke 14 coming alive.

Ultimately, Jesus was calling them to abandon themselves. They were leaving certainty for uncertainty, safety for danger, self-preservation for self-denunciation. In a world that prizes promoting oneself, they were following a teacher who told them to crucify themselves. And history tells us the result. Almost all of them would lose their lives because they responded to his invitation.

WHAT ABOUT US?

Let's put ourselves in the shoes of these eager followers of Jesus in the first century. What if I were the potential disciple being told to drop my nets? What if you were the man whom Jesus told to not even say good-bye to his family? What if we were told to hate our families and give up everything we had in order to follow Jesus?

This is where we come face to face with a dangerous reality. We *do* have to give up everything we have to follow Jesus. We *do* have to love him in a way that makes our closest relationships in this world look like hate. And it is entirely possible that he *will* tell us to sell everything we have and give it to the poor.

But we don't want to believe it. We are afraid of what it might mean for our lives. So we rationalize these passages away. "Jesus wouldn't really tell us not to bury our father or say good-bye to our family. Jesus didn't literally mean to sell all we have and give it to the poor. What Jesus really meant was…"

And this is where we need to pause. Because we are starting to redefine Christianity. We are giving in to the dangerous temptation to take the Jesus of the Bible and twist him into a version of Jesus we are more comfortable with.

A nice, middle-class, American Jesus. A Jesus who doesn't mind materialism and who would never call us to give away everything we have. A Jesus who would not expect us to forsake our closest relationships so that he receives all our affection. A Jesus who is fine with nominal devotion that does not infringe on our comforts, because, after all, he loves us just the way we are. A Jesus who wants us to be balanced, who wants us to avoid dangerous extremes, and who, for that matter, wants us to avoid danger altogether. A Jesus who brings us comfort and prosperity as we live out our Christian spin on the American dream.

But do you and I realize what we are doing at this point? We are molding Jesus into our image. He is beginning to look a lot like us because, after all, that is whom we are most comfortable with. And the danger now is that when we gather in our church buildings to sing and lift up our hands in worship, we may not actually be worshiping the Jesus of the Bible. Instead we may be worshiping ourselves.

THE COST OF NONDISCIPLESHIP

Dietrich Bonhoeffer, a German theologian struggling to follow Christ in the midst of Nazi rule, penned one of the great Christian books of the twentieth century. In it he wrote that the first call every Christian experiences is "the call to abandon the attachments of this world." The theme of the book is summarized in one potent sentence: "When Christ calls a man, he bids him come and die."[11] Bonhoeffer aptly entitled his book *The Cost of Discipleship*.

Based on what we have heard from Jesus in the Gospels, we would have to agree that the cost of discipleship is great. But I wonder if the cost of nondiscipleship is even greater.

The price is certainly high for people who don't know Christ and who live in a world where Christians shrink back from self-denying faith and settle into self-indulging faith. While Christians choose to spend their lives fulfilling the American dream instead of giving their lives to proclaiming the kingdom of God, literally billions in need of the gospel remain in the dark.

Just a few months before becoming a pastor, I stood atop a mountain in the heart of Hyderabad, India. This high point in the city housed a temple for Hindu gods. I smelled the offerings that had been given to the wooden gods behind me. I saw teeming masses in front of me. Every direction I turned, I glimpsed an urban center filled with millions upon millions of people.

And then it hit me. The overwhelming majority of these people had never even heard the gospel. They offer religious sacrifices day in and day out because no one has told them that, in Christ, the final sacrifice has already been offered on their behalf. As a result they live without Christ, and if nothing changes, they will die without him as well.

As I stood on that mountain, God gripped my heart and flooded my mind with two resounding words: "Wake up." Wake up and realize that there are infinitely more important things in your life than football and a 401(k). Wake up and realize there are real battles to be fought, so different from the superficial, meaningless "battles" you focus on. Wake up to the countless multitudes who are currently destined for a Christless eternity.

The price of our nondiscipleship is high for those without Christ. It is high also for the poor of this world.

Consider the cost when Christians ignore Jesus' commands to sell their possessions and give to the poor and instead choose to spend their resources on better comforts, larger homes, nicer cars, and more stuff. Consider the cost when these Christians gather in churches and choose to spend millions of dollars on nice buildings to drive up to, cushioned chairs to sit in, and endless programs to enjoy for themselves. Consider the cost for the starving multitudes who sit outside the gate of contemporary Christian affluence.

I remember when I was preparing to take my first trip to Sudan in 2004. The country was still at war, and the Darfur region in western Sudan had just begun to make headlines. A couple of months before we left, I received a Christian news publication in the mail. The front cover had two headlines side by side. I'm not sure if the editor planned for these particular headlines to be next to each other or if he just missed it in a really bad way.

On the left one headline read, "First Baptist Church Celebrates New $23 Million Building." A lengthy article followed, celebrating the church's expensive new sanctuary. The exquisite marble, intricate design, and beautiful stained glass were all described in vivid detail.

On the right was a much smaller article. The headline for it read, "Baptist Relief Helps Sudanese Refugees." Knowing I was about to go to Sudan, my attention was drawn. The article described how 350,000 refugees in western Sudan were dying of malnutrition and might not live to the end of the year. It briefly explained their plight and sufferings. The last sentence said that Baptists had sent money to help relieve the suffering of the Sudanese. I was excited until I got to the amount.

Now, remember what was on the left: "First Baptist Church Celebrates New $23 Million Building." On the right the article said, "Baptists have raised $5,000 to send to refugees in western Sudan."

Five thousand dollars.

That is not enough to get a plane into Sudan, much less one drop of water to people who need it.

Twenty-three million dollars for an elaborate sanctuary and five thousand dollars for hundreds of thousands of starving men, women, and children, most of whom were dying apart from faith in Christ.

Where have we gone wrong?

How did we get to the place where this is actually tolerable?

Indeed, the cost of nondiscipleship is great. The cost of believers not taking Jesus seriously is vast for those who don't know Christ and devastating for those who are starving and suffering around the world. But the cost of nondiscipleship is not paid solely by them. It is paid by us as well.

A Call to Treasure

Did you catch what Jesus said when he told the rich man to abandon his possessions and give to the poor? Listen again, particularly to the second half of Jesus' invitation: "Go, sell everything you have and give to the poor, *and you will have treasure in heaven.*"[12] If we are not careful, we can misconstrue these radical statements from Jesus in the Gospels and begin to think that he does not want the best for us. But he does. Jesus was not trying to strip this man of all his pleasure. Instead he was offering him the satisfaction of eternal treasure. Jesus was saying, "It will be better, not just for the poor, but for you too, when you abandon the stuff you are holding on to."

We see the same thing over in Matthew 13. There Jesus tells his disciples, "The kingdom of heaven is like treasure hidden in a field. When a man found it, he hid it again, and then in his joy went and sold all he had and bought that field."[13]

I love this picture. Imagine walking in a field and stumbling upon a treasure that is more valuable than anything else you could work for or find in this life. It is more valuable than all you have now or will ever have in the future.

You look around and notice that no one else realizes the treasure is here, so you cover it up quickly and walk away, pretending you haven't seen anything. You go into town and begin to sell off all your possessions to have enough money to buy that field. The world thinks you're crazy. "What are you thinking?" your friends and family ask you.

You tell them, "I'm buying that field over there."

They look at you in disbelief. "That's a ridiculous investment," they say. "Why are you giving away everything you have?"

You respond, "I have a hunch," and you smile to yourself as you walk away.

You smile because you know. You know that in the end you are not really giving away anything at all. Instead you are gaining. Yes, you are abandoning everything you have, but you are also gaining more than you could have in any other way. So with joy—with joy!—you sell it all, you abandon it all. Why? Because you have found something worth losing everything else for.

This is the picture of Jesus in the gospel. He is something—someone—worth losing everything for. And if we walk away from the Jesus of the gospel, we walk away from eternal riches. The cost of nondiscipleship is profoundly greater for us than the cost of discipleship. For when we abandon the trinkets of this world and respond to the radical invitation of Jesus, we discover the infinite treasure of knowing and experiencing him.

IS HE WORTH IT?

This brings us to the crucial question for every professing or potential follower of Jesus: Do we really believe he is worth abandoning everything for? Do you and I really believe that Jesus is so good, so satisfying, and so rewarding that we will leave all we have and all we own and all we are in order to find our fullness in him? Do you and I believe him enough to obey him and to follow him wherever he leads, even when the crowds in our culture—and maybe in our churches—turn the other way?

In this book I want to show you that, with the best of intentions, we have actually turned away from Jesus. We have in many areas blindly and unknowingly embraced values and ideas that are common in our culture but are antithetical to the gospel he taught. Here we stand amid an American dream dominated by self-advancement, self-esteem, and self-sufficiency, by individualism, materialism, and universalism. Yet I want to show you our desperate need to revisit the words of Jesus, to listen to them, to believe them, and to obey them. We need to return with urgency to a biblical gospel, because the cost of not doing so is great for our lives, our families, our churches, and the world around us.

As I mentioned previously, I have more questions than I have answers. And every day I see more disconnects between the Christ of Scripture and the Christianity that characterizes my life and the church God has entrusted me to lead. I have so far to go. We have so far to go.

But I want to know him. I want to experience him. I want to be part of a people who delight in him like the brothers and sisters in underground Asia who have nothing but him. And I want to be part of a people who are risking it all for him.

For the sake of more than a billion people today who have yet to even hear the gospel, I want to risk it all. For the sake of twenty-six thousand children who will die today of starvation or a preventable disease, I want to risk it all. For the sake of an increasingly marginalized and relatively ineffective church in our culture, I want to risk it all. For the sake of my life, my family, and the people who surround me, I want to risk it all.

And I am not alone. In the faith family I have the privilege to lead, I am joined by wealthy doctors who are selling their homes and giving to the poor or moving overseas; successful business leaders who are mobilizing their companies to help the hurting; young couples who have moved into the inner city to live out the gospel; and senior adults, stay-at-home moms, college students, and teenagers who are reorienting their lives around radical abandonment to Jesus. I'll introduce you to many of them in the course of this book.

There's nothing special about us. But we're proof that ordinary people who are naturally drawn to the comforts of the American dream can be converted to a radical faith in a radical Savior. Why not join us?

If you are serious about taking this journey, though, I believe a couple of preconditions exist. This goes back to the two big questions I started asking myself when I realized I was a megachurch leader trying to follow a minichurch leader.

First, from the outset you need to *commit to believe* whatever Jesus says. As a Christian, it would be a grave mistake to come to Jesus and say, "Let me hear what you have to say, and then I'll decide whether or not I like it." If you approach Jesus this way, you will never truly hear what he has to say. You have to say yes to the words of Jesus before you even hear them.

Then second, you need to *commit to obey* what you have heard. The gospel does not prompt you to mere reflection; the gospel requires a response. In the process of hearing Jesus, you are compelled to take an honest look at your life, your family, and your church and not just ask, "What is he saying?" but also ask, "What shall I do?"

In the pages to come, we will together explore the biblical gospel alongside our cultural assumptions with an aim toward embracing Jesus for who he really is, not for who we have created him to be. We will look at the core truth of a God-centered gospel and see how we have manipulated it into a human-centered (and ultimately dissatisfying) message. We will see a purpose for our lives that transcends the country and culture we live in, and we will see our desperate need for his presence to fulfill that purpose in us. We will discover that our meaning is found in community and our life is found in giving ourselves for the sake of others in the church, among the lost, and among the poor. We will evaluate where true security and safety are found in this world, and in the end we will determine not to waste our lives on anything but uncompromising, unconditional abandonment to a gracious, loving Savior who invites us to take radical risk and promises us radical reward.

CHAPTER TWO

TOO HUNGRY
FOR WORDS

**DISCOVERING THE TRUTH AND BEAUTY
OF THE GOSPEL**

Travel with me back to the underground house-church scene I
described in chapter 1. On my first day with these believers, they
simply asked me to lead a Bible study. "Please meet us tomorrow
at two o'clock in the afternoon."

So I put some thoughts together for a short Bible study and
went to the designated location, where about twenty house-church
leaders were waiting. I don't remember when we started, but I do
remember that eight hours later we were still going strong. We
would study one passage, and then they would ask about another.
This would lead to another topic, then to another, and by the end
of the day, our conversations had ranged from dreams and visions
to tongues and the Trinity.

It was late in the evening, and they wanted to continue
studying, but they needed to get back to their homes. So they

asked the two main church leaders and me, "Can we meet again tomorrow?"

I said, "I would be glad to. Shall we meet at the same time?"

They responded, "No, we want to start early in the morning."

I said, "Okay. How long would you like to study?"

They replied, "All day."

Thus began a process in which, over the next ten days, for eight to twelve hours a day, we would gather to study God's Word. They were hungry.

On the second day I introduced these relatively new believers to the story of Nehemiah. I gave them the background and history of this Bible book and showed them in Nehemiah 8 the importance of God's Word. Afterward we took a short break, and I saw the leaders talking intently about something in small groups. A few minutes later one of them approached me. "We have never learned any of this truth before, and we want to learn more," she said. Then she dropped the bomb. "Would you be willing to teach us about all the books of the Old Testament while you are here?"

I laughed. Smiling, I said, "All the Old Testament? That would take a long time."

By this time others were joining in the conversation, and they said, "We will do whatever it takes. Most of us are farmers, and we work all day, but we will leave our fields unattended for the next couple of weeks if we can learn the Old Testament."

So that's what we did. The next day I walked them through an overview of Old Testament history. Then we started in Genesis, and in the days that followed, we plowed through the highlights and main themes of every Old Testament book. Imagine teaching the Song of Songs to a group of Asian believers, many of whom have never read the book before, and just praying that they don't ask any questions!

On the next-to-last day, we finished in Malachi. I had twelve more hours to teach, and I had no clue what to say. Once you've taught Habakkuk, what else is there to cover?

So the last day I started teaching on a random subject. But within an hour I was interrupted by one of the leaders. "We have a problem," he said.

Worried that I had said something wrong, I responded, "What is the matter?"

He replied, "You have taught us the Old Testament, but you have not taught us the New Testament."

I smiled, but he was serious.

"We would like to learn the New Testament today," he said.

As other leaders across the room nodded, I had no choice. For the next eleven hours, we walked briskly from Matthew to Revelation.

Just imagine going to a worship gathering in one of those house churches. Not an all-day training in the Word. Just a normal three-hour worship service late in the evening. The Asian believer who is taking you gives you the instructions. "Put on dark pants and a jacket with a hood on it. We will put you in the back of our car and drive you into the village. Please keep your hood on and your face down."

When you arrive in the village under the cover of night,

another Asian believer meets you at the door of the car. "Follow me," he says.

With your hood over your head, you crawl out of the car, keeping your face toward the ground. You begin to walk with your eyes fixed on the feet of the man in front of you as he leads you down a long and winding path with a small flashlight. You hear more and more footsteps around you as you progress down the trail. Then finally you round the corner and walk into a small room.

Despite its size, sixty believers have crammed into it. They are all ages, from precious little girls to seventy-year-old men. They are sitting either on the floor or on small stools, lined shoulder to shoulder, huddled together with their Bibles in their laps. The roof is low, and one light bulb dangles from the middle of the ceiling as the sole source of illumination.

No sound system.

No band.

No guitar.

No entertainment.

No cushioned chairs.

No heated or air-conditioned building.

Nothing but the people of God and the Word of God.

And strangely, that's enough.

God's Word is enough for millions of believers who gather in house churches just like this one. His Word is enough for millions of other believers who huddle in African jungles, South American rain forests, and Middle Eastern cities.

But is his Word enough for us?

SECRET CHURCH

This is the question that often haunts me when I stand before a crowd of thousands of people in the church I pastor. What if we take away the cool music and the cushioned chairs? What if the screens are gone and the stage is no longer decorated? What if the air conditioning is off and the comforts are removed? Would his Word still be enough for his people to come together?

At Brook Hills we decided to try to answer this question. We actually stripped away the entertainment value and invited people to come together simply to study God's Word for hours at a time. We called it Secret Church.

We set a date—one Friday night—when we would gather from six o'clock in the evening until midnight, and for six hours we would do nothing but study the Word and pray. We would interrupt the six-hour Bible study periodically to pray for our brothers and sisters around the world who are forced to gather secretly. We would also pray for ourselves, that we would learn to love the Word as they do.

We weren't sure how many would show up that first evening, but by night's end about a thousand people had gathered. Our topic of study was the Old Testament. After our first try we decided to do it again, and again, and now we have to take reservations because we cannot contain all the people who want to come.

One of my favorite sights is to look across a room packed with people with their Bibles in their laps, studying who God is and what God has said—*after midnight* (we have never ended on time). Granted, we still have the cushioned chairs—though we did discuss the possibility of removing them! And we still have the comforts of a nice building with indoor bathrooms. But we are taking steps, I hope, toward discovering what it means to be a people who are hungry for the revelation of God.

What is it about God's Word that creates a hunger to hear more? And not just to hear the Word but to long for it, study it, memorize it, and follow it? What causes followers of Christ around the world literally to risk their lives in order to know it?

These questions cause us to step back and look at the foundations of the gospel. Fundamentally, the gospel is the revelation of who God is, who we are, and how we can be reconciled to him. Yet in the American dream, where self reigns as king (or queen), we have a dangerous tendency to misunderstand, minimize, and even manipulate the gospel in order to accommodate our assumptions and our desires. As a result, we desperately need to explore how much of our understanding of the gospel is American and how much is biblical. And in the process we need to examine whether we have misconstrued a proper response to the gospel and maybe even missed the primary reward of the gospel, which is God himself.

WHO HE REALLY IS

The gospel reveals the glory of God. According to God's Word, he is the sovereign Creator of all things. He knows all things, sustains all things, and owns all things. He is holy above all. He is righteous in all his ways, just in all his wrath, and loving toward all he has made.[1]

I wonder sometimes, though, if we intentionally or just unknowingly mask the beauty of God in the gospel by minimizing his various attributes. Peruse the Christian marketplace, and you will find a plethora of books, songs, and paintings that depict God as a loving Father. And he is that. But he is not *just* a loving Father, and limiting our understanding of God to this picture ultimately distorts the image of God we have in our culture.

Yes, God is a loving Father, but he is also a wrathful Judge. In his wrath he hates sin. Habakkuk prayed to God, "Your eyes are too pure to look on evil; you cannot tolerate wrong."[2] And in some sense, God also hates sinners. You might ask, "What happened to 'God hates the sin and loves the sinner'?" Well, the Bible happened to it. One psalmist said to God, "The arrogant cannot stand in your presence; you hate all who do wrong."[3] Fourteen times in the first fifty psalms we see similar descriptions of God's hatred toward sinners, his wrath toward liars, and so on. In the chapter in the gospel of John where we find one of the most famous verses concerning God's love, we also find one of the most neglected verses concerning God's wrath.[4]

The gospel reveals eternal realities about God that we would sometimes rather not face. We prefer to sit back, enjoy our clichés, and picture God as a Father who might help us, all the while ignoring God as a Judge who might damn us. Maybe this is why we fill our lives with the constant drivel of entertainment in our culture—and in the church. We are afraid that if we stop and really look at God in his Word, we might discover that he evokes greater awe and demands deeper worship than we are ready to give him.

But this is just the point. We are not ready to give him what he asks for because our hearts are set against him. God's revelation in the gospel not only reveals who he is, but it also reveals who we are.

Who We Really Are

An old preaching professor used to take his students to a cemetery every semester. Standing on the perimeter overlooking scores of headstones, he would ask his students in all sincerity to speak over the graves and call people from the ground to rise up and live. With some embarrassment and an awkward chuckle or two, they would try it. Of course, one by one they would fail. The professor would then look at his students and remind them of a core truth in the gospel: people are spiritually dead, just as those corpses in the cemetery were physically dead, and only words from God can bring them to spiritual life.

This is the reality about humanity. We are each born with an evil, God-hating heart. Genesis 8:21 says that every inclination of man's heart is evil from childhood, and Jesus' words in Luke 11:13 assume that we know we are evil. Many people say, "Well, I have always loved God," but the reality is, no one has. We may have loved a god that we made up in our minds, but the God of the Bible, we hate.

In our evil we rebel against God. We take the law of God, written in his Word and on our hearts, and we disobey it. This is the picture of the very first sin in Genesis 3. Even if God has said not to eat from the tree of knowledge, we are going to do it anyway.

We spurn our Creator's authority over us. God beckons storm

clouds, and they come. He tells the wind to blow and the rain to fall, and they obey immediately. He speaks to the mountains, "You go there," and he says to the seas, "You stop here," and they do it. Everything in all creation responds in obedience to the Creator...until we get to you and me. We have the audacity to look God in the face and say, "No."

Jesus told us that everyone who sins is a slave to sin, and Paul went so far as to say that we are captive to the devil himself.[5] And because we are slaves to sin, we are blinded to God's truth. Ephesians 4:18 says that we are darkened in our understanding and our hearts are like stone. According to 2 Corinthians 4:4, we can't even see Christ because of the depth of our spiritual blindness.

The Bible describes us as enemies of God and objects of his wrath. We are spiritually dead and eternally separated from God.[6] What's worse is that we can do nothing to change our status before God. No one who is morally evil can choose good, no man who is a slave can set himself free, no woman who is blind can give herself sight, no one who is an object of wrath can appease that wrath, and no person who is dead can cause himself to come to life.

The gospel confronts us with the hopelessness of our sinful condition. But we don't like what we see of ourselves in the gospel, so we shrink back from it. We live in a land of self-improvement. Certainly there are steps we can take to make ourselves better. So we modify what the gospel says about us.

We are not evil, we think, and certainly not spiritually dead. Haven't you heard of the power of positive thinking? I can become a better me and experience my best life now. That's why God is there—to make that happen. My life is not going right, but God loves me and has a plan to fix my life. I simply need to follow certain steps, think certain things, and check off certain boxes, and then I am good.

Both our diagnosis of the situation and our conclusion regarding the solution fit nicely in a culture that exalts self-sufficiency, self-esteem, and self-confidence. We already have a fairly high view of our morality, so when we add a superstitious prayer, a subsequent dose of church attendance, and obedience to some of the Bible, we feel pretty sure that we will be all right in the end.

Note the contrast, however, when you diagnose the problem biblically. The modern-day gospel says, "God loves you and has a wonderful plan for your life. Therefore, follow these steps, and you can be saved." Meanwhile, the biblical gospel says, "You are an enemy of God, dead in your sin, and in your present state of rebellion, you are not even able to see that you need life, much less to cause yourself to come to life. Therefore, you are radically dependent on God to do something in your life that you could never do."

The former sells books and draws crowds. The latter saves souls. Which is more important?

In the gospel God reveals the depth of our need for him. He shows us that there is absolutely nothing we can do to come to him. We can't manufacture salvation. We can't program it. We can't produce it. We can't even initiate it. God has to open our eyes, set us free, overcome our evil, and appease his wrath. He has to come to us.

Now we are getting to the beauty of the gospel.

WHAT (OR WHOM) WE REALLY NEED

I remember sitting outside a Buddhist temple in Indonesia. Men and women filled the elaborate, colorful temple grounds, where they daily performed their religious rituals. Meanwhile, I was engaged in a conversation with a Buddhist leader and a Muslim leader in this particular community. They were discussing how all religions are fundamentally the same and only superficially different. "We may have different views about small issues," one of them said, "but when it comes down to essential issues, each of our religions is the same."

I listened for a while, and then they asked me what I thought. I said, "It sounds as though you both picture God (or whatever you call god) at the top of a mountain. It seems as if you believe that we are all at the bottom of the mountain, and I may take one route up the mountain, you may take another, and in the end we will all end up in the same place."

They smiled as I spoke. Happily they replied, "Exactly! You understand!"

Then I leaned in and said, "Now let me ask you a question. What would you think if I told you that the God at the top of the mountain actually came down to where we are? What would you think if I told you that God doesn't wait for people to find their way to him, but instead he comes to us?"

They thought for a moment and then responded, "That would be great."

I replied, "Let me introduce you to Jesus."

This is the gospel. As long as you and I understand salvation as checking off a box to get to God, we will find ourselves in the meaningless sea of world religions that actually condemn the human race by exalting our supposed ability to get to God. On the other hand, when you and I realize that we are morally evil, dead in sin, and deserving of God's wrath with no way out on our own, we begin to discover our desperate need for Christ.

Our understanding of who God is and who we are drastically affects our understanding of who Christ is and why we need him. For example, if God is only a loving Father who wants to help his people, then we will see Christ as a mere example of that love. We will view the Cross as just a demonstration of God's love in which he allowed Roman soldiers to crucify his Son so that sinful man would know how much he loves us.

But this picture of Christ and the Cross is woefully inadequate, missing the entire point of the gospel. We are not saved from our sins because Jesus was falsely tried by Jewish and Roman officials and sentenced by Pilate to die. Neither are we saved because Roman persecutors thrust nails into the hands and feet of Christ and hung him on a cross.

Do we really think that the false judgment of men heaped upon Christ would pay the debt for all of humankind's sin? Do we really think that a crown of thorns and whips and nails and a wooden cross and all the other facets of the crucifixion that we glamorize are powerful enough to save us?

Picture Christ in the Garden of Gethsemane. As he kneels before his Father, drops of sweat and blood fall together from his head. Why is he in such agony and pain? The answer is not because he is afraid of crucifixion. He is not trembling because of what the Roman soldiers are about to do to him.

Since that day countless men and women in the history of Christianity have died for their faith. Some of them were not just hung on crosses; they were burned there. Many of them went to their crosses singing.

One Christian in India, while being skinned alive, looked at his persecutors and said, "I thank you for this. Tear off my old garment, for I will soon put on Christ's garment of righteousness."

As he prepared to head to his execution, Christopher Love wrote a note to his wife, saying, "Today they will sever me from my physical head, but they cannot sever me from my spiritual head, Christ." As he walked to his death, his wife applauded while he sang of glory.

Did these men and women in Christian history have more courage than Christ himself? Why was he trembling in that garden, weeping and full of anguish? We can rest assured that he was not a coward about to face Roman soldiers. Instead he was a Savior about to endure divine wrath.

Listen to his words: "My Father, if it is possible, may this cup be taken from me." The "cup" is not a reference to a wooden cross; it is a reference to divine judgment. It is the cup of God's wrath.[7]

This is what Jesus is recoiling from in the garden. All God's holy wrath and hatred toward sin and sinners, stored up since the beginning of the world, is about to be poured out on him, and he is sweating blood at the thought of it.

What happened at the Cross was not primarily about nails

being thrust into Jesus' hands and feet but about the wrath due your sin and my sin being thrust upon his soul. In that holy moment, all the righteous wrath and justice of God due us came rushing down like a torrent on Christ himself. Some say, "God looked down and could not bear to see the suffering that the soldiers were inflicting on Jesus, so he turned away." But this is not true. God turned away because he could not bear to see your sin and my sin on his Son.

One preacher described it as if you and I were standing a short hundred yards away from a dam of water ten thousand miles high and ten thousand miles wide. All of a sudden that dam was breached, and a torrential flood of water came crashing toward us. Right before it reached our feet, the ground in front of us opened up and swallowed it all. At the Cross, Christ drank the full cup of the wrath of God, and when he had downed the last drop, he turned the cup over and cried out, "It is finished."

This is the gospel. The just and loving Creator of the universe has looked upon hopelessly sinful people and sent his Son, God in the flesh, to bear his wrath against sin on the cross and to show his power over sin in the Resurrection so that all who trust in him will be reconciled to God forever.

RADICAL REVELATION TO BE RADICALLY RECEIVED

So how do we respond to this gospel? Suddenly contemporary Christianity sales pitches don't seem adequate anymore. Ask Jesus to come into your heart. Invite Jesus to come into your life. Pray this prayer, sign this card, walk down this aisle, and accept Jesus as your personal Savior. Our attempt to reduce this gospel to a shrink-wrapped presentation that persuades someone to say or pray the right things back to us no longer seems appropriate.

That is why none of these man-made catch phrases are in the Bible. You will not find a verse in Scripture where people are told to "bow your heads, close your eyes, and repeat after me." You will not find a place where a superstitious sinner's prayer is even mentioned. And you will not find an emphasis on accepting Jesus.[8] We have taken the infinitely glorious Son of God, who endured the infinitely terrible wrath of God and who now reigns as the infinitely worthy Lord of all, and we have reduced him to a poor, puny Savior who is just begging for us to accept him.

Accept him? Do we really think Jesus needs our acceptance? Don't *we* need *him?*

I invite you to consider with me a proper response to this gospel. Surely more than praying a prayer is involved. Surely more than religious attendance is warranted. Surely this gospel evokes unconditional surrender of all that we are and all that we have to all that he is.

You and I desperately need to consider whether we have ever truly, authentically trusted in Christ for our salvation. In this light Jesus' words at the end of the Sermon on the Mount are some of the most humbling in all Scripture.

Not everyone who says to me, "Lord, Lord," will enter the kingdom of heaven, but only he who does the will of my Father who is in heaven. Many will say to me on that day,

"Lord, Lord, did we not prophesy in your name, and in your name drive out demons and perform many miracles?" Then I will tell them plainly, "I never knew you. Away from me, you evildoers!"[9]

Jesus was not speaking here to irreligious people, atheists, or agnostics. He was not speaking to pagans or heretics. He was speaking to devoutly religious people who were deluded into thinking they were on the narrow road that leads to heaven when they were actually on the broad road that leads to hell. According to Jesus, one day not just a few but many will be shocked—eternally shocked—to find that they were not in the kingdom of God after all.

The danger of spiritual deception is real. As a pastor, I shudder at the thought and lie awake at night when I consider the possibility that scores of people who sit before me on a Sunday morning might think they are saved when they are not. Scores of people who have positioned their lives on a religious road that makes grandiose promises at minimal cost. We have been told all that is required is a one-time decision, maybe even mere intellectual assent to Jesus, but after that we need not worry about his commands, his standards, or his glory. We have a ticket to heaven, and we can live however we want on earth. Our sin will be tolerated along the way. Much of modern evangelism today is built on leading people down this road, and crowds flock to it, but in the end it is a road built on sinking sand, and it risks disillusioning millions of souls.

Biblical proclamation of the gospel beckons us to a much different response and leads us down a much different road. Here the gospel demands and enables us to turn from our sin, to take up our cross, to die to ourselves, and to follow Jesus. These are the terms and phrases we see in the Bible. And salvation now consists of a deep wrestling in our souls with the sinfulness of our hearts, the depth of our depravity, and the desperation of our need for his grace. Jesus is no longer one to be accepted or invited in but one who is infinitely worthy of our immediate and total surrender.

You might think this sounds as though we have to earn our way to Jesus through radical obedience, but that is not the case at all. Indeed, "it is by grace you [are] saved, through faith—and this not from yourselves, it is the gift of God—not by works, so that no one can boast."[10] We are saved from our sins by a free gift of grace, something that only God can do in us and that we cannot manufacture ourselves.

But that gift of grace involves the gift of a new heart. New desires. New longings. For the first time, we want God. We see our need for him, and we love him. We seek after him, and we find him, and we discover that he is indeed the great reward of our salvation. We realize that we are saved not just to be forgiven of our sins or to be assured of our eternity in heaven, but we are saved to know God. So we yearn for him. We want him so much that we abandon everything else to experience him. This is the only proper response to the revelation of God in the gospel.

This is why men and women around the world risk their lives to know more about him. This is why we must avoid cheap caricatures of Christianity that fail to exalt the revelation of God in his Word. This is why you and I cannot settle for anything less than a God-centered, Christ-exalting, self-denying gospel.

Give Us a Hunger

I pray continually for this kind of hunger in the church God has given me to lead and in churches spread across our country's landscape. I pray that we will be a people who refuse to gorge our spiritual stomachs on the entertaining pleasures of this world, because we have chosen to find our satisfaction in the eternal treasure of his Word. I pray that God will awaken in your heart and mine a deep and abiding passion for the gospel as the grand revelation of God.

As I look at my e-mails today, I smile. One is from a woman I do not know in Las Vegas. Yesterday she sat on a plane with a member of our faith family in Birmingham. This member is a salesman for a pharmaceutical company. She tells me that throughout the flight he was reading his Bible carefully. She describes the intensity that was evident on his face. She struck up a conversation with him, and in her words "his eyes teared up" as he talked about his passion for Christ and his desire to know him more. She asked him what church he was a part of, and she has sent me this e-mail to encourage me.

Another e-mail is from a college student who recently went to a crowded church event. She writes with gentleness about her disappointment when the preacher in the gathering virtually ignored God's Word. Though a large crowd was present and everything seemed to be successful, she noticed a glaring void. She concludes, "I'm at a point now where if preachers can't come up with something other than inspirational speeches, then maybe they should just read from the Word for their sermon. The Spirit is good to work with just that." I'm certainly not the best preacher, and I definitely don't want to lead people to be critical of other preachers, but I do delight in hearing a college student say she really wants the revelation of God.

The third e-mail is from a member of our faith family who attended Secret Church not long ago. The topic that night was "Who is God?" and we explored the glory of God's attributes. The man decided this word about God was too good to keep to himself. So he writes me from Uganda, where he is teaching the doctrine of God to church members and leaders there. He is not a staff member or a paid minister; he is simply a man in love with God's Word. He writes, "Pastor, for ten hours a day, I am preaching my heart out by his grace! We have sat for hours talking through the Word, and God has spoken with such a mighty hand of truth that I can't even begin to tell you about it all now! Praise the glorious name of Christ—he is being exalted a continent away!"

The revelation of God in the gospel is good. I invite you to receive it. Maybe to trust in the Christ of the gospel for the first time and for the first time to receive a new heart, a heart that is not only cleansed of sin but that now longs for him. Or maybe simply to recover a passion for God's Word—his radical revelation of himself—and discover once again the reward that is found in simply knowing and experiencing him.

CHAPTER THREE

BEGINNING AT THE
END OF OURSELVES

I was in Indonesia, the country with the largest Muslim population in the world, teaching in an Indonesian seminary. Before they graduate, the students in this seminary are required to plant a church, with at least thirty new, baptized believers, in a Muslim community. I spoke at their commencement ceremony, and as the graduates walked across the stage, I was captivated by the humble yet confident look on their faces. Every one of them had fulfilled the church-planting requirement. The most solemn part of the day was a moment of silence for two of their classmates who had died at the hands of Muslim persecutors.

It was a privilege getting to know these students and listening to their stories. One brother, Raden, shared his testimony. With a fiery look in his eye and an intense tone in his voice, he said, "Before I became a Christian, I was a fighter. I learned ninja, jujitsu, and a variety of other techniques for taking people down."

I nodded. I was making a mental note: *Don't mess with Raden.*

He continued, "One day I was sharing the gospel in an unreached village with people who had never heard of Jesus. I was in one house sharing Christ with a family, and the witch doctor from the village came to the house." Witch doctors and magic men are common in villages like these. They hold sway over entire communities with their curses and incantations.

"The witch doctor called me out," Raden said. "He wanted me to fight him." Raden smiled as he confessed, "My first thought was to walk out there and take the witch doctor down. But when I turned to go outside, the Lord told me that I no longer need to do the fighting. God would do the fighting for me."

So Raden walked outside, pulled up a chair, and sat down in front of the witch doctor. He told his challenger, "I don't do the fighting. My God does the fighting for me."

Raden recounted what happened next. "As the witch doctor attempted to speak, he began to gasp for air. He was choking and couldn't breathe. People came running to see what was wrong, and within a few minutes the witch doctor had fallen over dead."

By now the entire village had crowded around the scene. Raden said, "I had never seen anything like this, and I didn't know what to do. But then I thought, *I guess this is a good time to preach the gospel.*" Raden smiled and said, "So that's what I did, and many people in that village trusted in Christ for the first time that day."

Now, I'm not recommending this as a new church-growth

methodology. Making pronouncements on people that lead to their deaths just doesn't seem to be the best way to go about things. But this story was a clear reminder to me that two thousand years ago when believers proclaimed the name of Jesus, it caused the blind to see, the lame to walk, and the dead to rise. The name of Jesus had the power to cause evil spirits to flee and to bring the most hardened hearts to God. And the reality is, two thousand years later the power of Jesus' name is still great.

The question for us, then, is whether we trust in his power. And the problem for us is that in our culture we are tempted at every turn to trust in our own power instead. So the challenge for us is to live in such a way that we are radically dependent on and desperate for the power that only God can provide.

SUBTLE DANGERS

To this point, we have seen how the American dream radically differs from the call of Jesus and the essence of the gospel. This differentiation is heightened when we contrast trust in the power of God with reliance on our own abilities.

As the American dream goes, we can do anything we set our minds to accomplish. There is no limit to what we can accomplish when we combine ingenuity, imagination, and innovation with skill and hard work. We can earn any degree, start any business, climb any ladder, attain any prize, and achieve any goal. James Truslow Adams, who is credited with coining the phrase "American dream" in 1931, spoke of it as "a dream...in which each man and each woman shall be able to attain to the fullest stature of which they are innately capable, and be recognized by others for what they are."[1]

So is there anything wrong with this picture? Certainly hard work and high aspirations are not bad, and the freedom to pursue our goals is something we should celebrate. Scripture explicitly commends all these things. But underlying this American dream are a *dangerous assumption* that, if we are not cautious, we will unknowingly accept and a *deadly goal* that, if we are not careful, we will ultimately achieve.

The dangerous assumption we unknowingly accept in the American dream is that our greatest asset is our own ability. The American dream prizes what people can accomplish when they believe in themselves and trust in themselves, and we are drawn toward such thinking. But the gospel has different priorities. The gospel beckons us to die to ourselves and to believe in God and to trust in his power. In the gospel, God confronts us with our utter inability to accomplish anything of value apart from him. This is what Jesus meant when he said, "I am the vine; you are the branches. If a man remains in me and I in him, he will bear much fruit; apart from me you can do nothing."[2]

Even more important is the subtly fatal goal we will achieve when we pursue the American dream. As long as we achieve our desires in our own power, we will always attribute it to our own glory. To use Adams's words, we will be "recognized by others for what [we] are." This, after all, is the goal of the American dream: to make much of ourselves. But here the gospel and the American dream are clearly and ultimately antithetical to each other. While the goal of the American dream is to make much of us, the goal of the gospel is to make much of God.

EXALTING OUR INABILITY

In direct contradiction to the American dream, God actually delights in exalting our inability. He intentionally puts his people in situations where they come face to face with their need for him. In the process he powerfully demonstrates his ability to provide everything his people need in ways they could never have mustered up or imagined. And in the end, he makes much of his own name.[3]

Consider the story of Joshua outside Jericho, a strong city with massive walls surrounding it. Certainly Joshua was anxious about leading the people of God in his first battle as commander. I can only imagine the sense of inadequacy he felt as he contemplated the task before him.

That's why, at the end of Joshua 5, we see him alone, wondering about the combat that lies ahead. But suddenly God appears. In that moment God promises Joshua that his side will win the battle, and he gives Joshua the plans.

You can almost picture Joshua as he listens, thinking, *What will it be? A frontal assault? A trick of some kind? Or just lay a siege and starve them out?*

Put yourself in Joshua's shoes as you hear these battle plans:

March around the city once with all the armed men. Do this for six days. Have seven priests carry trumpets of rams' horns in front of the ark. On the seventh day, march around the city seven times, with the priests blowing the trumpets. When you hear them sound a long blast on the trumpets, have all the people give a loud shout; then the wall of the city will collapse and the people will go up, every man straight in.[4]

Let's be honest. That's weird. If you're Joshua, you're wanting a second opinion at this point.

Why did God design this battle plan for taking the first city in the Promised Land? Don't miss what God was doing. He was divinely orchestrating the events of his people so that in the end only he could get the glory for what would happen. Read the rest of Joshua 6, and you will see them take the city of Jericho just as God had outlined. But notice carefully what you *don't* see. You don't see all the Israelites going up to the trumpet players and telling them what an incredible job they did that day. I can almost hear them now: "Abishai, I've never heard you play that well." "Nimrod, when you hit the high C, that was beautiful, man." No. Instead you see the people of Israel realizing that only God could have done this.

This is how God works. He puts his people in positions where they are desperate for his power, and then he shows his provision in ways that display his greatness.

DEPENDENT ON OURSELVES OR DESPERATE FOR HIS SPIRIT?

This is where I am most convicted as a pastor of a church in the United States of America. I am part of a system that has created a whole host of means and methods, plans and strategies for doing church that require little if any power from God. And it's not just pastors who are involved in this charade. I am concerned that all of us—pastors and church members in our culture—have blindly embraced an American dream mentality that emphasizes our abilities and exalts our names in the ways we do church.

Consider what it takes for successful businessmen and businesswomen, effective entrepreneurs and hardworking associates, shrewd retirees and idealistic students to combine forces with a creative pastor to grow a "successful church" today. Clearly, it doesn't require the power of God to draw a crowd in our culture. A few key elements that we can manufacture will suffice.

First, we need a good performance. In an entertainment-driven culture, we need someone who can captivate the crowds. If we don't have a charismatic communicator, we are doomed. So even if we have to show him on a video screen, we must have a good preacher. It's even better if he has an accomplished worship leader with a strong band at his side.

Next, we need a place to hold the crowds that will come, so we gather all our resources to build a multimillion-dollar facility to house the performance. We must make sure that all facets of the building are excellent and attractive. After all, that's what our culture expects. Honestly, that's what *we* expect.

Finally, once the crowds get there, we need to have something to keep them coming back. So we need to start programs—first-class, top-of-the-line programs—for kids, for youth, for families, for every age and stage. In order to have these programs, we need professionals to run them. That way, for example, parents can simply drop off their kids at the door, and the professionals can handle ministry for them. We don't want people trying this at home.

I know this may sound oversimplified and exaggerated, but are these not the elements we think of when we consider growing, dynamic, successful churches in our day? I get fliers on my desk every day advertising entire conferences built around creative communication, first-rate facilities, innovative programs, and entrepreneurial leadership in the church. We Christians are living out the American dream in the context of our communities of faith. We have convinced ourselves that if we can position our resources and organize our strategies, then in church as in every other sphere of life, we can accomplish anything we set our minds to.

But what is strangely lacking in the picture of performances, personalities, programs, and professionals is desperation for the power of God. God's power is at best an add-on to our strategies. I am frightened by the reality that the church I lead can carry on most of our activities smoothly, efficiently, even successfully, never realizing that the Holy Spirit of God is virtually absent from the picture. We can so easily deceive ourselves, mistaking the presence of physical bodies in a crowd for the existence of spiritual life in a community.

A DIFFERENT PICTURE

But when I open the book of Acts in the New Testament and observe the picture of the church there, I see such different images. I see a small band of timid disciples huddled together in an upper room. They know they need God's power. They are Galileans, disrespected by the higher classes in Jerusalem as lower-class, rural, uneducated commoners. This is the group that the spread of Christianity depends on. So what are they doing? They are not plotting strategies. They are "joined together constantly in prayer."[5] They are not busy putting their faith in themselves or relying on themselves. They are pleading for the power of God, and they are confident that they are not going to accomplish anything without his provision.

Then God sends his Spirit in power, and everything changes. These uneducated Galileans start speaking the gospel in a multiplicity of languages that everyone can understand. The crowds are shocked, and Peter stands up to preach Christ. Peter, who just weeks before was afraid to admit he even knew Jesus, now stands under the power of God in front of thousands of people, proclaiming Jesus. More than three thousand people are saved.

Talk about church growth. Acts 1 started with about a hundred and twenty believers, and now in Acts 2 there are more than three thousand. If you do the math, that's almost 2500 percent growth…in a day.

The story continues. People are coming to Christ every hour. In Acts 3, Peter and John speak the name of Jesus, and a forty-year-old man crippled from birth stands up to walk for the first time. In Acts 4, they pray until the building where they are gathered begins to shake. In a telling commentary, Luke says, "When [the crowds] saw the courage of Peter and John and realized that they were unschooled, ordinary men, they were astonished and they took note that these men had been with Jesus."[6]

It only gets better from there. In Acts 5, the apostles are performing "many miraculous signs and wonders among the people."[7] The sick are being healed of their diseases, and evil spirits are being cast out. In Acts 6 and 7, the danger the disciples are experiencing is increasing, and so is God's power among them. By chapter 8, the church is scattering to Judea and Samaria, preaching the gospel everywhere they go. Philip gets zapped by the Holy Spirit from one place to another to lead an Ethiopian to Christ. In Acts 9, Saul, the persecutor of Christians, becomes a follower of Christ. In Acts 10, racial and ethnic barriers to the spread of the gospel begin to collapse, and in Acts 11, the church at Antioch is founded as the future base of mission to the nations. In Acts 12, as Peter sits on death row in a jail cell, the church prays, and suddenly Peter's chains fall off. He practically sleepwalks out of prison. Acts 13 launches Paul into his travels from city to city, preaching the gospel, healing people of diseases, casting out demons, and even raising people from the dead.

What I love about the picture that unfolds in Acts is the intentional way Luke (the author of Acts) makes much of God in the way he tells the story. Listen to the language in Acts 2 when Luke records the results of Peter's sermon at Pentecost. He writes, "Those who accepted his message were baptized, and about three thousand were added to their number that day" (verse 41). Did you hear the passive language? They *were added.* It begs the question "Who added them?" Go down to verse 47 in the same chapter, and Luke makes sure we get the right answer. There he writes, "*The Lord* added to their number daily those who were being saved."

The trend continues. Acts 5:14 says, "More and more men and women believed in the Lord and *were added* to their number." When Barnabas shares the gospel in Antioch, the result is that "a great number of people *were brought* to the Lord" (11:24). Later, in Pisidian Antioch, a host of Gentiles "who *were appointed* for eternal life believed" (13:48).

This is the design of God among his people. He is giving unlikely people his power so it is clear who deserves the glory for the success that takes place.

The story of the church continues throughout the rest of the New Testament, and as I read it, I cannot help but long to be a part of this kind of scene in the church today. A scene where we refuse to operate in a mind-set dominated by an American dream that depends on what we can achieve with our own abilities. A scene where we no longer settle for what we can do in our own power. A scene where the church radically trusts in God's great power to provide unlikely people with unlimited, unforeseen, uninhibited resources to make his name known as great. I want to be a part of *that* dream.

SUPERIOR POWER

When I was considering becoming the pastor of the faith family I now lead, I thought and even said to other people, "This church has so many resources—so many gifts, so many talents, so many leaders, so much money. If this church could get behind a global purpose, it could shake the nations for the glory of God."

I have since discovered that this was a woefully wrongheaded way to think. The reality is that it doesn't matter how many resources the church has. The church I lead could have all the man-made resources that one could imagine, but apart from the power of the Holy Spirit, such a church will do nothing of significance for the glory of God.

In fact, I believe the opposite is true. The church I lead could have the least gifted people, the least talented people, the fewest leaders, and the least money, and this church under the power of the Holy Spirit could still shake the nations for his glory. The reality is that the church I lead can accomplish more during the next month in the power of God's Spirit than we can in the next hundred years apart from his provision. His power is so superior to ours. Why do we not desperately seek it?

ORDINARY CHRISTIANS, EXTRAORDINARY GOD

Consider the implications for Christianity in America if this is true. What if God in all his might is simply waiting to show his power in a people who turn their backs on a philosophy of life that exalts their supposed ability to do anything they want and who instead confess their desperate need for him? What if God in all his grace is radically committed to showing himself strong on behalf of a people who express their need for him so their lives might make much of him?

This is the story of George Muller. (We have so much to learn from church history.) Muller (1805–98) pastored a church in Bristol, England, for more than sixty years, but he was best known for the orphan ministry he began. During his life he cared for more than ten thousand orphans. Remarkably, and intentionally, he never asked for money or other resources to provide for these orphans. Instead he simply prayed and trusted God to provide.

When I read Muller's biography, I was shocked to learn why he started the orphanage. His primary purpose was not to care for orphans. Instead, he wrote in his journal:

> If I, a poor man, simply by prayer and faith, obtained without asking any individual, the means for establishing and carrying on an Orphan-House, there would be something which, with the Lord's blessing, might be instrumental in strengthening the faith of the children of God, besides being a testimony to the consciences of the unconverted, of the reality of the things of God. This, then, was *the primary reason* for establishing the Orphan-House.… The *first and primary object* of the work was (and still is:) that God might be magnified by the fact, that the orphans under my care are provided with all they need, only by prayer and faith without anyone being asked by me or my fellow-laborers whereby it may be seen, that God is faithful still, and hears prayer still.[8]

Muller decided that he wanted to live in such a way that it would be evident to all who looked at his life—Christian and non-Christian alike—that God is indeed faithful to provide for his people. He risked his life trusting in the greatness of God, and in the end his life made much of the glory of God.

God delights in using ordinary Christians who come to the end of themselves and choose to trust in his extraordinary provision. He stands ready to allocate his power to all who are radically dependent on him and radically devoted to making much of him.

GOD OUR FATHER

I love to provide for my children. I'm writing this from a train in India on my way back home, and I can't wait to see them. I can't wait to give my sons a huge hug, wrestle with them on the floor, and tell them about all I've seen in India. And, of course, I'm looking forward to giving them gifts I've brought from overseas.

They expect these things from me. Not just gifts, but also the love and affection I show them. They expect them, and they need them. I don't mean that in an unhealthy way, and I don't presume that if something happened to me, they would be lost without me. I'm not needed in that way. But I am their dad. I love providing for them, and they know how much I love them by the ways I provide for them. The more they look to me for that love and find it, the more they trust in me as their dad.

This relationship with my sons helps me understand Luke 11. Listen to what Jesus says there: "Which of you fathers, if your son asks for a fish, will give him a snake instead? Or if he asks for an egg, will give him a scorpion? If you then, though you are evil, know how to give good gifts to your children, how much more will your Father in heaven give the Holy Spirit to those who ask him!"[9] The context of Luke 11 is Jesus' teaching on prayer. He is saying that when we pray for the Father's provision, we will find that his provision is good. And the more he provides for us, the more we will trust him as our Father.

But the last part of this passage is where I have always been confused. You see, Jesus makes a similar statement over in Matthew 7, where he says, "If you, then, though you are evil, know how to give good gifts to your children, how much more will your Father in heaven give good gifts to those who ask him!"[10] Did you notice the difference there at the end? In Luke, our Father in heaven will give *the Holy Spirit* to us when we ask him. In Matthew, our Father will give *good gifts* to us when we ask him. To me, the Matthew version makes more sense. When we pray, God gives us good gifts, just as an earthly father gives good gifts to his children.

But why does Luke 11 refer to the Father giving the Holy Spirit? To be honest with you, I used to think, *What if I wasn't asking for the Holy Spirit? What if I was asking for something else? Why does Jesus say the Father gives the Holy Spirit in response to our prayers?*

The answer to this question uncovers the beauty of the Spirit of God in our lives.

Think about it this way. Maybe you are going through a struggle in your life. A tragedy strikes you or someone close to you, and you are hurting. So you go to God in prayer, and you ask him to comfort you. Do you realize what God does? He doesn't give you comfort. Instead he gives you the Holy Spirit, who is called the Comforter.[11] The Holy Spirit literally comes to dwell in you and puts the very comfort of Christ inside you as you walk through your pain.

Suppose another time you are making a big decision in your

life, and you need help. You have a couple of different options
before you, and you need guidance to decide which way is best.
So you ask God for help. But he doesn't answer with guidance.
Instead he answers by sending the Holy Spirit, who is our Guide.[12]
God sends the Helper, who will live in you and not only tell you
what decision to make but also enable you to make that decision.

Yet another time you need discernment, and God gives you
the Spirit of wisdom. At other times you need strength, and God
gives you the Spirit of power. Still other times you ask God for
love, joy, peace, patience, kindness, goodness, faithfulness, gentleness, or self-control, and he gives you the Spirit, who makes all
these things a reality in your life.[13]

The Holy Spirit is the Comforter, the Helper, the Guide, the
very presence of God living in you.

This is the great promise of God in prayer. We ask God for
gifts in prayer, and he gives us the Giver. We ask God for supply,
and he gives us the Source. We ask God for money, and he doesn't
give us cash; instead, so to speak, he gives us the bank!

When you really contemplate it, this seems bold, doesn't it?
To go to God and say, "God, I know you are busy running the
universe and keeping all of creation alive, but I have this problem
in my life. And, God, I don't really want comfort for the moment,
and I don't really want guidance for the moment. Would you…
would you just come down, live in me, and walk through this for
me?" Isn't it pushing the envelope to ask the God of the universe
to come down and take residence in you and me?

What Jesus is saying, though, is that God our Father delights
in this. He delights in giving us himself. He puts his very power

in us so we might have all we need to accomplish his purposes in this world. This is the heart of Jesus' promise to his disciples in John 14, the promise that precedes his promises about the Holy Spirit: "I tell you the truth, anyone who has faith in me will do what I have been doing. He will do even greater things than these, because I am going to the Father. And I will do whatever you ask in my name, so that the Son may bring glory to the Father. You may ask me for anything in my name, and I will do it."[14]

Do you think Jesus really means this? Even greater things than he did? Anything we ask?

Jesus absolutely means this. Now, this is not a genie-in-a-bottle approach to God that assumes he is ready to grant our every wish. But it is a rock-solid promise that the resources of heaven are ready and waiting for the people of God who desire to make much of him in this world. For the people of God who long to see his power at work and who live to see his purposes accomplished, he will give us absolutely everything we need according to his very presence alive in us.

ON OUR KNEES

If we are not careful, we will completely bypass this promise and miss out on the power of God's presence. Surrounded by the self-sufficiency of American culture, we can convince ourselves that we have what it takes to achieve something great. In our churches we can mimic our culture, planning and programming, organizing and strategizing, creating and innovating—all in an effort that will show what we can accomplish in our own ability. As Adams said, we can "attain to the fullest stature of which [we] are innately capable, and be recognized by others for what [we] are." But there is another way.

It is the way of Christ. Instead of asserting ourselves, we crucify ourselves. Instead of imagining all the things we can accomplish, we ask God to do what only he can accomplish. Yes, we work, we plan, we organize, and we create, but we do it all while we fast, while we pray, and while we constantly confess our need for the provision of God. Instead of dependence on ourselves, we express radical desperation for the power of his Spirit, and we trust that Jesus stands ready to give us everything we ask for so that he might make much of our Father in the world.

Think about it. Would you say that your life is marked right now by desperation for the Spirit of God? Would you say that the church you are a part of is characterized by this sense of desperation?

Why would we ever want to settle for Christianity according to our ability or settle for church according to our resources? The power of the one who raised Jesus from the dead is living in us, and as a result we have no need to muster up our own might. Our great need is to fall before an almighty Father day and night and to plead for him to show his radical power in and through us, enabling us to accomplish for his glory what we could never imagine in our own strength. And when we do this, we will discover that we were created for a purpose much greater than ourselves, the kind of purpose that can only be accomplished in the power of his Spirit.

CHAPTER FOUR

THE GREAT WHY
OF GOD

GOD'S GLOBAL PURPOSE FROM
THE BEGINNING TILL TODAY

I remember exactly where I was sitting.

It was in a home where leaders of an American church had gathered—a church that had demonstrated great kindness to me in the past, praying for me and even sending me financial support (completely unsolicited). The pastor sat immediately to my right, and a couple of deacons were on the other side of the den. This was a Saturday evening, and I had been invited to preach the following morning in their church.

As we sat around the den, they asked me questions about how my wife and I were doing. I shared with them about inner-city ministry in New Orleans, where we were living at the time. I told them about ministry in housing projects ridden with poverty and gang violence. I told them about ministry among homeless men and women who struggled with various addictions.

Then I told them about ministry opportunities God had recently given me around the world. I told them about people's receptivity to the gospel in places that are traditionally hostile to Christianity. I told them that, whether in the inner city or overseas, God was drawing people to himself in some of the toughest areas of the world.

Expecting them to share in my excitement, I paused to listen for their response. After an awkward silence, one of the deacons leaned forward in his chair, looked at me, and said, "David, I think it's great you are going to those places. But if you ask me, I would just as soon God annihilate all those people and send them to hell."

That's exactly what he said. I was shocked and speechless. I had no idea what to say in response. I wish I had said something, but I'm still not sure what I would have said. Annihilate them? Send them to hell?

After a moment of silence, the rest of the room resumed conversation as if nothing out of the ordinary had just happened.

It got worse.

The next morning we arrived at the church building, and the worship service began. The pastor rose to welcome everyone, and during his introductory remarks he began talking about how thankful he was to be living in the United States. I am not sure what sparked the rousing patriotic address that followed, but for the next few minutes he told the church that there was no chance he would ever live anywhere else in the world. *Amen*s were firing left and right from the crowd. Engulfed in nationalistic zeal, I was just waiting for Lee Greenwood to burst into song in the background.

Minutes later I got up to preach on going to all nations with the gospel. When I finished, I walked down to the front while the pastor got up to close the service. These were his words: "Brother David, we are so excited about all that God is doing in New Orleans and in all nations, and we are excited that you are serving there." He continued, "And, brother, we promise that we will continue to send you a check so we don't have to go there ourselves."

He wasn't finished.

"I remember a time at my last congregation when a missionary from Japan came to speak," he said. "I told that church that if they didn't give financial support to this missionary, I was going to pray that God would send their kids to Japan to serve with that missionary."

Wow.

Did the pastor just threaten his congregation with the punishment of going to the world?

He continued, "And my church gave that man a laptop and a whole lot of money."

Apparently the threat worked.

The service was dismissed, and my wife and I climbed into the car to drive home. I could hardly believe the things I had heard. A range of emotions consumed me—anger, sadness, disappointment, confusion. But as I began to process what had happened over the last twenty-four hours, I was struck by a frightening realization.

Could it be that this deacon and this pastor expressed what most professing Christians in America today believe but are not bold enough to say? This may sound a bit harsh, but consider the reality.

How many of us are embracing the comforts of suburban America while we turn a deaf ear to inner cities in need of the gospel? How many of us are so settled in the United States that we have never once given serious thought to the possibility that God may call us to live in another country? How often are we willing to give a check to someone else as long as we don't have to go to the tough places in the world ourselves? How many of us parents are praying that God will raise up our children to leave our homes and go overseas, even if that means they may never come back? And how many of us are devoting our lives to taking the gospel to people in hostile regions around the world where Christians are not welcomed? Certainly few of us would be so bold as to say we "would just as soon God annihilate all those people and send them to hell," but if we do not take the gospel to them, isn't that where they will go?

Meanwhile, Jesus commands us to go. He has created each of us to take the gospel to the ends of the earth, and I propose that anything less than radical devotion to this purpose is unbiblical Christianity.

ENJOY HIS GRACE, EXTEND HIS GLORY

Consider why God formed us in the first place. As the self-sufficient God of the universe, he certainly had no unmet need in himself, so why did he create us? The last thing I want to do is to presume to know exhaustively the mind and motives of God. Nor do I want to oversimplify his ways. But it seems that God tells us why he made us. There is a twofold purpose evident from the beginning of history.

On one hand, we were created by God to enjoy his grace. Apart from everything else God created, we were made in his image.[1] We alone have the capacity to enjoy God in intimate relationship with him. The first word the Bible uses to describe that relationship is *blessing*. God blessed the human race, not because of any merit or inherent worth in us, but simply out of pure, unadulterated grace. God created humankind to enjoy his grace.

But that was not the end of the story, because on the other hand, God immediately followed his blessing with a command. "God blessed them and said to them, 'Be fruitful and increase in number; fill the earth and subdue it.'"[2] God gave his people his image for a reason—so that they might multiply his image throughout the world. He created human beings, not only to enjoy his grace in a relationship with him, but also to extend his glory to the ends of the earth.

Simple enough. Enjoy his grace and extend his glory. This is the twofold purpose behind the creation of the human race in Genesis 1, and it sets the stage for an entire Book that revolves around the same purpose. In every genre of biblical literature and every stage of biblical history, God is seen pouring out his grace on his people for the sake of his glory among all peoples.

In Genesis 12, God forms his people by saying to Abraham, "I will make you into a great nation and I will bless you; I will make your name great, and you will be a blessing." Then God connects his promise to Abraham with a deeper purpose: "All peoples on earth will be blessed through you."³ God blesses Abraham abundantly but not ultimately for Abraham's sake. He blesses Abraham so that Abraham might be the conduit of God's blessing to all the peoples of the earth. God tells Abraham to enjoy his grace as Abraham extends God's glory.

Consider the self-exalting purpose of God in the redemption of his people from slavery in Egypt. Immediately following the Exodus, God led them to the shore of the Red Sea, with the Egyptians on their heels and nowhere else to turn. Listen to the motive of God as he says, "I will gain glory for myself through Pharaoh and all his army, and the Egyptians will know that I am the LORD."⁴ He miraculously parted the waters, led his people through the middle on dry land, and then caused the waves to swallow up the Egyptians in the Israelites' rearview mirrors for one primary reason: to gain glory for himself. The Egyptians and all the nations after them knew that he is the Lord and he saves his people. God blessed his people in a miraculous way so that his salvation would be made known among all peoples.

Consider another Old Testament story, that of Shadrach, Meshach, and Abednego. Why would a God of love let these three Hebrew men be thrown into a fiery furnace? Is this how God treats those who risk everything for him? How does this make you feel about the next time you are faced with taking a stand for God? We read the story and are fascinated by it, but we rarely get to the end to see the point.

> Then Nebuchadnezzar said, "Praise be to the God of
> Shadrach, Meshach and Abednego, who has sent his angel

and rescued his servants! They trusted in him and defied the king's command and were willing to give up their lives rather than serve or worship any god except their own God. Therefore I decree that the people of any nation or language who say anything against the God of Shadrach, Meshach and Abednego be cut into pieces and their houses be turned into piles of rubble, for no other god can save in this way."[5]

The very king who declared that everybody should bow down to him was now declaring that anybody who spoke against God should be cut into pieces! The reason God let these guys be thrown into a fiery furnace was so that they would come out on the other side without a drop of sweat on their brows and so that this pagan king would declare that the God of Shadrach, Meshach, and Abednego is worthy of praise in all nations and languages. God really is in the business of blessing his people in unusual ways so his goodness and his greatness will be declared among all peoples.

Verses that reiterate this truth abound throughout the Old Testament. Psalms, for example, speaks of God guiding his people for his name's sake and blessing his people so that his ways would be made known in all nations. The prophets beautifully depict the mercy of God toward his people so that they would witness to the nations that he is Lord.[6]

Ezekiel 36 contains some of the most startling words from the mouth of God as he recounts his work among his people. God is addressing how the people of Israel had sinned against him, and he describes the reason for what he did among them.

> This is what the Sovereign LORD says: It is not for your
> sake, O house of Israel, that I am going to do these things,
> but for the sake of my holy name, which you have pro-
> faned among the nations where you have gone. I will
> show the holiness of my great name, which has been pro-
> faned among the nations, the name you have profaned
> among them. Then the nations will know that I am the
> LORD, declares the Sovereign LORD, when I show myself
> holy through you before their eyes.[7]

What a statement! God goes so far as to say that when he acts among his people, he doesn't show his grace, mercy, and justice for their sake but for the sake of his own holy name among the nations.

The global purpose of God evident in the history, writings, and prophets of the Old Testament carries over into the New Testament. In the Gospels we see how Jesus ended his time on earth by commanding his followers to take the gospel to the ends of the earth.[8] The letters are filled with the same emphasis as Paul, Peter, James, and John led the church through persecution and suffering to spread the glory of God to the nations.

In light of all we have seen, it is no surprise to get to the last book of the Bible and see the culmination of God's purpose. Imagine this scene described by John:

> After this I looked and there before me was a great multi-
> tude that no one could count, from every nation, tribe,
> people and language, standing before the throne and in

front of the Lamb. They were wearing white robes and were holding palm branches in their hands. And they cried out in a loud voice:

"Salvation belongs to our God,
who sits on the throne,
and to the Lamb."[9]

In the beginning of earthly history, God's purpose was to bless his people so that all peoples would glorify him for his salvation. Now, at the end, God's purpose is fulfilled. Individuals from every nation, tribe, people, and language are bowing down around the throne of God and singing praises to the one who has blessed them with salvation. This is the final, ultimate, all-consuming, glorious, guaranteed, overwhelmingly global purpose of God in Scripture. It is the great why of God.

God blesses his people with extravagant grace so they might extend his extravagant glory to all peoples on the earth. This basic, fundamental truth permeates Scripture from beginning to end. Yet I wonder if we unknowingly ignore the great why of God.

JESUS DIDN'T DIE FOR JUST YOU

We live in a church culture that has a dangerous tendency to disconnect the grace of God from the glory of God. Our hearts resonate with the idea of enjoying God's grace. We bask in sermons, conferences, and books that exalt a grace centering on us. And while the wonder of grace is worthy of our attention, if that grace is disconnected from its purpose, the sad result is a self-centered Christianity that bypasses the heart of God.

If you were to ask the average Christian sitting in a worship service on Sunday morning to summarize the message of Christianity, you would most likely hear something along the lines of "The message of Christianity is that God loves me." Or someone might say, "The message of Christianity is that God loves me enough to send his Son, Jesus, to die for me."

As wonderful as this sentiment sounds, is it biblical? Isn't it incomplete, based on what we have seen in the Bible? "God loves me" is not the essence of biblical Christianity. Because if "God loves me" is the message of Christianity, then who is the object of Christianity?

God loves *me.*

Me.

Christianity's object is *me.*

Therefore, when I look for a church, I look for the music that best fits *me* and the programs that best cater to *me* and *my* family. When I make plans for *my* life and career, it is about what works best for *me* and *my* family. When I consider the house I will live in, the car I will drive, the clothes I will wear, the way I will live, I will choose according to what is best for *me.* This is the version of Christianity that largely prevails in our culture.

But it is not biblical Christianity.

The message of biblical Christianity is not "God loves me, period," as if we were the object of our own faith. The message of biblical Christianity is "God loves me so that I might make him— his ways, his salvation, his glory, and his greatness—known among all nations." Now God is the object of our faith, and Christianity centers around him. We are not the end of the gospel; God is.

God centers on himself, even in our salvation. Remember his words in Ezekiel: he saves us, not for our sake, but for the sake of his holy name. We have received salvation so that his name will be proclaimed in all nations. God loves us for his sake in the world.

This may come as a shock to us. You mean that God has an ulterior motive in blessing us? We are not the end of his grace? And the answer Scripture gives is clear. Indeed, we are not at the center of his universe. God is at the center of his universe, and everything he does ultimately revolves around him.

If this is true, we may wonder, then does this make God selfish? How can God's purpose be to exalt himself? This is a good question, and it causes us to pause until we ask the follow-up question: Whom else would we have him exalt? At the very moment God exalted someone or something else, he would no longer be the great God worthy of all glory in all the universe, which he is.

We must guard against misunderstanding here. The Bible is not saying that God does not love us deeply. On the contrary, we have seen in Scripture a God of unusual, surprising, intimate passion for his people. But that passion does not ultimately center on his people. It centers on his greatness, his goodness, and his glory being made known globally among all peoples. And to disconnect God's blessing from God's global purpose is to spiral downward into an unbiblical, self-saturated Christianity that misses the point of God's grace.

It's a foundational truth: God creates, blesses, and saves each of us for a radically global purpose. But if we are not careful, we will be tempted to make exceptions. We will be tempted to adopt spiritual smoke screens and embrace national comforts that excuse us from the global plan of Christ. And in the process we will find ourselves settling for lesser plans that the culture around us—and even the church around us—deems more admirable, more manageable, and more comfortable.

"I'M NOT CALLED"

I wonder if we have in some ways intentionally and in other ways unknowingly erected lines of defense against the global purpose God has for our lives. It's not uncommon to hear Christians say, "Well, not everyone is called to foreign missions," or more specifically, "I am not called to foreign missions." When we say this, we are usually referring to foreign missions as an optional program in the church for a faithful few who apparently are called to that. In this mind-set, missions is a compartmentalized program of the church, and select folks are good at missions and passionate about missions. Meanwhile, the rest of us are willing to watch the missions slide shows when the missionaries come home, but in the end God has just not called most of us to do this missions thing.

But where in the Bible is missions ever identified as an optional program in the church? We have just seen that we were all created by God, saved from our sins, and blessed by God to make his glory known in all the world. Indeed, Jesus himself has not merely called us to go to all nations; he has created us and commanded us to go to all nations. We have taken this command, though, and reduced it to a calling—something that only a few people receive.

I find it interesting that we don't do this with other words from Jesus. We take Jesus' command in Matthew 28 to make disciples of all nations, and we say, "That means other people." But we look at Jesus' command in Matthew 11:28, "Come to me, all you who are weary and burdened, and I will give you rest," and we say, "Now, that means me." We take Jesus' promise in Acts 1:8 that the Spirit will lead us to the ends of the earth, and we say, "That means some people." But we take Jesus' promise in John 10:10 that we will have abundant life, and we say, "That means me."

In the process we have unnecessarily (and unbiblically) drawn a line of distinction, assigning the *obligations* of Christianity to a few while keeping the *privileges* of Christianity for us all. In this way we choose to send off other people to carry out the global purpose of Christianity while the rest of us sit back because we're "just not called to that."

Now, we know that each of us has different gifts, different skills, different passions, and different callings from God. God has gifted you and me in different ways. This was undoubtedly the case with the disciples. Peter and Paul had different callings. James and John had different callings. However, each follower of Christ in the New Testament, regardless of his or her calling, was intended to take up the mantle of proclaiming the gospel to the ends of the earth. That's the reason why he gave each of them his Spirit and why he gave them all the same plan: make disciples of all nations.

Isn't it the same today? When I sit down for lunch with Steve, a businessman in our faith family, it's obvious we have different callings in our lives. He's an accountant; I'm a pastor. He is gifted with numbers; I can't stand numbers. But we both understand that God has called us and gifted us for a global purpose. So Steve is constantly asking, "How can I lead my life, my family, and my accounting firm for God's glory in Birmingham and around the world?" He is leading co-workers to Christ; he is mobilizing accountants to serve the poor; and his life is personally impacting individuals and churches in Latin America, Africa, and Eastern Europe with the gospel.

Steve and others like him have decided that they are not going to take the command of Christ to make disciples of all nations and label it a calling for a few. They are not going to sit on the sidelines while a supposed special class of Christians accomplishes the global purpose of God. They are convinced that God has created them to make his glory known in all nations, and they are committing their lives to accomplishing that purpose.

In Romans 1:14–15, Paul talks about being a debtor to the nations. He literally says, "I am in debt to Jews and Gentiles." The language is profound. Paul is saying that he owes a debt to every lost person on the face of the planet. Because he is owned by Christ, he owes Christ to the world.

Every saved person this side of heaven owes the gospel to every lost person this side of hell. We owe Christ to the world—to the least person and to the greatest person, to the richest person and to the poorest person, to the best person and to the worst person. We are in debt to the nations. Encompassed with this debt, though, in our contemporary approach to missions, we have subtly taken ourselves out from under the weight of a lost and dying world, wrung our hands in pious concern, and said, "I'm sorry. I'm just not called to that."

The result is tragic. A majority of individuals supposedly saved from eternal damnation by the gospel are now sitting back and making excuses for not sharing that gospel with the rest of the world.

But what if we don't need to sit back and wait for a call to foreign missions? What if the very reason we have breath is because we have been saved for a global mission? And what if anything less than passionate involvement in global mission is actually selling God short by frustrating the very purpose for which he created us?

"What About the Needs Here?"

Maybe the most common response that arises among Christians regarding the global purpose of God is "What about the needs here? Why do we need to be involved in other nations when there are so many needs in our nation?"

Among Christians in Birmingham (where I pastor), I often hear this statement phrased something like this: "I don't need to go to all nations, because God has given me a heart for the United States." Others might say, "God has given me a heart for Birmingham." These statements sound spiritual, but when we probe deeper, they seem more like smoke screens.

They are smoke screens because most of us really are not very concerned about the needs right around us. Most Christians rarely share the gospel, and most Christians' schedules are not heavily weighted to feeding the hungry, helping the sick, and strengthening the church in the neediest places in our country.

But even if we were doing these things, we would still be overlooking a foundational biblical truth when we say our hearts are for the United States. As we have seen all over Scripture, God's heart is for the world. So when we say we have a heart for the United States, we are admitting that we have a meager 5 percent of God's heart, and we are proud of it. When we say we have a heart for the city we live in, we confess that we have less than 1 percent of God's heart.

Certainly there are great needs here. But must we insist on dividing the Great Commission into an either-or proposition? Who told us that we had to choose to have a heart for the United States *or* a heart for the world? Based on the purpose of God we've seen in Scripture, shouldn't every Christian's heart be ultimately consumed with how we can make God's glory known in all the world?

It's 6,783,421,727 and counting. As I write this chapter, this is the population of the world. According to the most liberal estimates, approximately one-third of the world is Christian. These estimates include all who identify themselves as Christian, whether religiously, socially, or politically. Likely, not all of them are actually followers of Christ. But even if we assume they are, that still leaves 4.5 billion people who, if the gospel is true, at this moment are separated from God in their sin and (assuming nothing changes) will spend an eternity in hell.

Again, *4.5 billion.*

And most of them live outside the United States.

In light of all that we have seen in Scripture, certainly God has given us his grace to extend his glory not just to areas of need here but to areas of need around the world. Not either here or there, but both here and there.

In all this missions talk, you may begin to think, *Well, surely you're not suggesting that we're all supposed to move overseas.* That is certainly not what I'm suggesting (though I'm not completely ruling it out!). But this is precisely the problem. We have created the idea that if you have a heart for the world and you are passionate about global mission, then you move overseas. But if you have a heart for the United States and you are not passionate about global mission, then you stay here and support those who go. Meanwhile, flying right in the face of this idea is Scripture's claim that regardless of where we live—here or overseas—our hearts should be consumed with making the glory of God known in all nations.

I know there are probably some folks in the church I pastor who wouldn't mind if I left and lived in another nation. I say this kiddingly (I hope!), but, after all, isn't that where people who are passionate about the world go? But this is exactly why the church I pastor is stuck with me (as long as they'll have me). Because from cover to cover the Bible teaches that all the church—not just select individuals, but all the church—is created to reflect all the glory of God to all the world. Because every single man, woman, and child in the church I pastor is intended to impact nations for the glory of Christ, and there is a God-designed way for us to live our lives here, and do church here, for the sake of people around the world who don't know Christ.

So what is this God-designed way to live? All this talk about having a heart for the world may sound a bit cliché and even seem a bit hollow, so what does it really mean to live for the glory of Christ in all nations? As we continue to look at the words of Christ, we're going to dive into specific answers to this question. At this point let me give you just a few examples of individuals who have traded in the American dream for a dream that extends far beyond the country and culture in which they live.

A GREATER DREAM

Imagine the American dream in action.

Imagine a university student preparing for his profession. All his life he has been told to work hard at school so he can go to college, get a degree, and build a career. With the right amount of motivation, dedication, and intuition, he can make something of himself one day. So he presses on toward that goal.

Or imagine a gifted businessman who has reached his aspirations. He started with humble roots and faced daunting challenges, but he persevered through long days at the office and short nights at home to get to the top. He arrived there faster than he expected, and though it was not always easy, in the end he believes it was worth it. He now lives in an expansive suburban home with his wife and children, a self-made man with all he needs.

And then there is the married couple beginning retirement. Finally the wait is over, and the options abound. Settle into a quiet, secluded home, or travel across the country? Renovate the house, or take out a second mortgage on one in the mountains? Buy a fishing boat, or take up golf lessons? The pleasures they now enjoy are a monument to the years of toil and labor that have made it all possible.

Imagine these common scenarios and then ask the question, "Were we created for something much greater than this?"

Let me introduce you to Daniel, a college student like the one I mentioned earlier. He is a member of our faith family and a recent honor graduate with a degree in mechanical engineering from a nearby university. Coming out of school, he was given two attractive offers: take an extremely high-paying job at a nuclear power plant, or have all his expenses paid to complete master's and doctorate degrees in engineering.

Taking either one of these offers would certainly not have been bad, but two years ago Daniel came to faith in Christ. The focus of his entire life shifted to using the grace of God in his life to make much of the glory of God. Consequently, he turned down both options before him and instead went to work with an engineering program designed to help impoverished communities around the world. His dad e-mailed me soon after Daniel made this decision, saying, "Daniel has made a very radical departure from my long-held and traditional value system. I have raised my children with solid Christian values and naturally have expected them to grab the brass ring of opportunity and settle into a productive family life." In the rest of the e-mail, though, his dad described how proud he was that his son had let go of the pursuits of this world in order to "take the gospel to places and peoples unknown to him." And God has been faithful to Daniel. I met with him in my office a few weeks ago, and he told me about unprecedented opportunities that God is now giving him from America to Africa to Asia as he pursues a much greater dream than he ever had before.

And let me introduce you to Jeff, a businessman like the one I mentioned earlier, who climbed the ladder of success, only to realize that success in the kingdom of God involves moving down, not up. As a young professional, he scaled the heights of success in our culture in almost every conceivable way. I'll let him tell his story in his own words in excerpts from a speech he gave to other executives in his company during one of their conferences.

> My career has been a complete whirlwind in ways more successful than I ever anticipated it could be. I am paying more in taxes than I ever expected to make in a full year! I have been incredibly blessed. I was able to bring my wife home from work. Then we purchased our dream home in the exact neighborhood where we always wanted to live. I purchased the BMW; I bought the big beach house; and we went on great vacations. On top of all this, I was growing a business that I truly loved in an industry that I am passionate about. But somehow something was missing from my life, and I couldn't figure out what it was. I have been a Christian since I was seven years old, but through my pursuit of business and success, I somehow had replaced seeking the Lord with pursuing stuff and success.
>
> Then something happened last year that changed my life. I stood in a city dump in Tegucigalpa, Honduras. I saw men, women, and children who were living in a

dump where they scoured for food and shelter. Humbled by the reality of parents raising their kids in a dump, I reached my breaking point when I saw a woman eight months pregnant walk by me, looking for food. I couldn't decide which was worse—the fact that the baby was conceived in a dump or that it was going to be born there. In the middle of this scene, God asked me, "What are you going to do with what I have given you? How are you going to use your influence, your leadership, and your resources in the world around you?"

For the first time, Jeff realized that God had a purpose for his life that was greater than the pursuit of the next and bigger thing. So Jeff decided to walk away from the American dream. He still runs his business and makes a lot of money but not to make much of himself. He and a couple of other guys in our faith family have begun a ministry that works with local churches around the world to provide clean water in communities where thousands are dying every day of preventable waterborne diseases. Together they are discovering what we talked about in the last chapter: God is committed to providing abundant resources in support of those who are living according to his purpose.

Finally, let me introduce you to Ed and Patty. Now in their early seventies, they were presented with a plethora of options for what to do together in their retirement. In response, they chose an uncommon path. This year, between July and October, Ed and Patty were home a total of only eleven days. They weren't home, because they were doing disaster relief in cities and towns that had experienced flooding in the United States. They both went to Nigeria, and Ed went to Sri Lanka, where he cooked meals for the hungry in the middle of rebel fighting. Ed told me that Patty usually travels with him, but she doesn't like sleeping under trucks in the middle of rebel fighting, so she didn't go to Sri Lanka with him! Ed said to me one time, "What else am I going to do with my retirement? I just want to tell as many people about the gospel as I can."

If you were to meet Daniel, Jeff, Ed, or Patty, you might not see anything extraordinary about them. These are unassuming people who have achieved varying levels of success in this world. But all of them have this in common: They believe they were created for more than a Christian spin on the American dream. They believe the purpose of their lives is deeper than having a nice job, raising a decent family, living a comfortable life, and tacking church attendance onto the end of it. They believe Jesus has called them to a much higher plane and given them a much greater dream. They believe God has shown them great grace in order that he might use them to accomplish the glorious, global, God-exalting purpose that has been primary since the beginning of time, and they don't want to settle for anything less than radical abandonment to that purpose.

IMPACT THE WORLD

So what might this look like in your life? As we explore what it means to be radically abandoned to Christ, I invite you simply to let your heart be gripped, maybe for the first time, by the biblical prospect that God has designed a radically global purpose for your life. I invite you to throw aside gospel-less reasoning that might prevent you from accomplishing that purpose. I invite you to consider with me what it would mean for all of us—pastors and church members, businessmen and businesswomen, lawyers and doctors, consultants and construction workers, teachers and students, on-the-go professionals and stay-at-home moms—to spend all of our lives for the sake of all of God's glory in all of the world.

It sounds idealistic, I know. Impact the world. But doesn't it also sound biblical? God has created us to accomplish a radically global, supremely God-exalting purpose with our lives. The formal definition of *impact* is "a forcible contact between two things," and God has designed our lives for a collision course with the world.

And what if this is not only biblical but possible? There is an old maxim that those who say it can't be done should get out of the way of those who are doing it. What if a global, God-exalting, passionate idealism is exactly what is needed in the lives of individual Christians today? What if these radical Christians joined together in communities of faith called churches that were surrendered to the purpose for God's people that has been primary from the beginning of time? Maybe, just maybe, together we would see the accomplishment of that purpose.

I will close with an e-mail I recently received from Jamie, a mom in our faith family who had just returned from Guatemala. Another church had asked her to come and tell about her experience, and this is a portion of what she shared.

I made the decision to go to Guatemala after seeing in God's Word that he commands us to go and make disciples of all nations. I was going out of obedience, not because I had a heart for missions or a passion for the people of Guatemala. I want you to understand that I'm a wife, mother, and part-time psychologist—I'm not a missionary, and I'm certainly not a preacher. I was just being minimally obedient to what I believed God's Word tells all of us to do. Praise God he isn't minimally faithful and doesn't minimally bless us.

After spending a week around precious children who eat a small cup of porridge a day, the question I have come back to Birmingham asking God is why he has blessed me when others have so little. And this is what God has shown me: "I have blessed you for my glory. Not so you will have a comfortable life with a big house and a nice car. Not so you can spend lots of money on vacations, education, or clothing. Those aren't bad things, but I've blessed you so that the nations will know me and see my glory."

All my life I have completely disconnected God's blessings from God's purpose, and now I realize what I had never seen. God has blessed me to show his love to Domingo [an elderly man whom Jamie saw come to Christ in Guatemala that week]. God has blessed me to show his mercy and grace to children in Guatemala. That is why God has given me income and education and resources. God saves me so that the nations will know him. He blesses me so that all the earth will see his glory!

CHAPTER FIVE

THE MULTIPLYING
COMMUNITY

HOW ALL OF US JOIN TOGETHER
TO FULFILL GOD'S PURPOSE

On a scorching November day, I was sitting in the middle of the vast African landscape, sipping hot tea with my friend Bullen. We were surrounded by damaged buildings in a land ravaged by twenty years of civil war. What used to be a thriving community in Sudan was now seared and saddened. Thousands upon thousands of Bullen's brothers and sisters in Christ had died around him at the hands of a militant Muslim regime. And they were our brothers and sisters too.

Bullen had been separated from his family as a child and had grown up in Sudan on his own. But as I looked across at his dark, slender face on that day, I was struck by the contagious smile that shone whenever he spoke.

We were talking about how God had worked in Bullen's life, bringing him to trust in Christ when he could trust in nothing else. We discussed what God was doing in each of our lives, and we talked about the plans God had for us in the future. In the middle of that conversation, Bullen lowered the cup of hot tea from his lips, looked me in the eyes, and said, "David, I am going to impact the world."

An interesting statement. Here was a guy in the African bush with almost no resources. A guy who hadn't seen much of the world beyond the villages that surrounded him. A guy who by all outward appearances did not have much hope of changing his lot in life.

"Bullen, how are you going to impact the world?" I asked.

"I'm going to make disciples of all nations," he said.

"So you are going to impact the world by making disciples of all nations?"

That grin immediately spread across his face. "Why not?" he asked. Then he went back to sipping his tea.

I'll never forget those two words.

Why not?

As I lay down that night beneath the thatched roof of a mud hut, I could not get Bullen's question out of my mind. He had asked it with such innocent, idealistic passion. He was not only optimistic enough to think that he could actually affect the world around him, but he was also confident enough to know how he was going to do it. He really believed that in obeying Jesus' command to make disciples, he was going to impact the world.

In this chapter I want to propose that the plan Bullen identified for his life is the same plan that Jesus identified for each of our lives. Regardless of what country we live in, what skills we possess, what kind of education we have, or what kind of salary we make, Jesus has commanded each of us to make disciples, and *this is the means* by which we will impact the world. Indeed, Jesus has invited us to join with him in the surprisingly simple journey of spreading the gospel to all nations by spending our lives for the good of others and the glory of God.

The Next Step

In the last chapter we saw our need to connect the blessing of God with the purpose of God. I am indebted to mentors and colleagues, pastors and authors who have helped me understand the global, God-centered nature of God.

At the same time, I am concerned about a general vagueness that has existed in contemporary Christianity regarding the next step. We have seen that God blesses us so that his glory might be made known in all nations. But an all-important question remains. *How* do we make God's glory known in all nations? If God has given us his grace so that we might take his gospel to the ends of the earth, then *how* do we do that? Do we walk out into the streets and just start proclaiming the glory of God somehow? Should we all go to other nations? If we go, what do we do when we get there? What does all this look like in our day-to-day lives?

Jesus has much to teach us here. If we were left to ourselves with the task of taking the gospel to the world, we would immediately begin planning innovative strategies and plotting elaborate schemes. We would organize conventions, develop programs, and create foundations. We would get the biggest names to draw the biggest crowds to the biggest events. We would start megachurches and host megaconferences. We would do…well, we would do what we are doing today.

But Jesus is so different from us. With the task of taking the gospel to the world, he wandered through the streets and byways of Israel looking for a few men. Don't misunderstand me—Jesus was anything but casual about his mission. He was initiating a revolution, but his revolution would not revolve around the masses or the multitudes. Instead it would revolve around a few men. It would not revolve around garnering a certain position. Instead it would revolve around choosing a few people. He would intentionally shun titles, labels, plaudits, and popularity in his plan to turn the course of history upside down. All he wanted was a few men who would think as he did, love as he did, see as he did, teach as he did, and serve as he did. All he needed was to revolutionize the hearts of a few, and they would impact the world.

JESUS' GREAT GAMBLE

Picture Jesus as he prepares to go to the cross. Praying to the Father, he recounts his ministry in the world. He begins, "I have brought you glory on earth by completing the work you gave me to do."[1] Then he describes that work.

What is shocking is that when Jesus summarizes his work on earth, he doesn't start reliving all the great sermons he preached and all the people who came to listen to him. He doesn't talk about the amazing miracles he performed—giving sight to the blind, enabling the lame to walk, and feeding thousands of people with minimal food. He doesn't even mention bringing the dead back to life. Instead he talks repeatedly about the small group of men God had given him out of the world. They were the work God had given to him. They were, quite literally, his life.

When you read through John 17, you cannot help but sense the intensity of the affection Jesus had for this band of disciples and the gravity of the investment he had made in their lives. Consider this sampling from Jesus' prayer to his Father regarding his disciples:

- "I have revealed you to those whom you gave me out of the world."
- "All I have is yours, and all you have is mine. And glory has come to me through them."
- "While I was with them, I protected them and kept them safe by that name you gave me."
- "I am coming to you now, but I say these things while I am still in the world, so that they may have the full measure of my joy within them."
- "For them I sanctify myself, that they too may be truly sanctified."[2]

Jesus lived for them. During his earthly ministry, he spent more time with these twelve men than with everyone else in the world put together. This is astonishing when you really think about it. At the end of the Son of God's time on earth, he had staked everything on his relationships with twelve men. In the middle of his prayer, he even mentioned that one of them (Judas) was lost. So now we are down to eleven. These eleven guys were the small group responsible for carrying on everything Jesus had begun.

After his prayer in the upper room, Jesus went to the cross and died there. Then he rose from the grave and appeared to his disciples. One of his final moments with them is captured in Matthew 28. The eleven gathered around him, and Jesus said, "All authority in heaven and on earth has been given to me. Therefore go and make disciples of all nations, baptizing them in the name of the Father and of the Son and of the Holy Spirit, and teaching them to obey everything I have commanded you. And surely I am with you always, to the very end of the age."[3]

After intentionally spending his life on earth with these eleven men, Jesus told them, "Now you go out and do the same with others." The megastrategy of Jesus: make disciples.

ANY AND EVERY FOLLOWER OF CHRIST

Any Christian can do this. You don't need to have inordinate skill or unusual abilities to make disciples. You don't need to be a successful pastor or a charismatic leader to make disciples. You don't need to be a great communicator or an innovative thinker to make disciples. That's why Jesus says every Christian must do this.

One of the unintended consequences of contemporary church strategies that revolve around performances, places, programs, and professionals is that somewhere along the way people get left out of the picture. But according to Jesus, people are God's method for winning the world to himself. People who have been radically transformed by Jesus. People who are not sidelined to sit in a chair on Sundays while they watch professionals take care of ministry for them. People who are equipped on Sundays to participate in ministry every day of the week. People who are fit and free to do precisely what Jesus did and what Jesus told us to do. Make disciples.

People like Jim and Cathy. They sit on the front row in our worship gathering every week, but they are not sidelined in the church. They run a business and see their workplace as a platform for making disciples. Last year sixteen of their co-workers came to faith in Christ. And they are not obeying Christ just in the United States. Jim provides small-business training for men in impoverished Tanzania, while Cathy trains Tanzanian women in trades they can develop in their homes. Jim recently told me, "It really doesn't get any better than this. My heart overflows with praise that God chooses to work in me and my family."

Or people like Robert, a successful businessman in our community. After a recent study we went through on making disciples, Robert told me that in all his years in church he had never seen the responsibility—and privilege—he had to impact nations for the glory of Christ. So now he's doing it. Robert and his wife currently host a small group in their home every week where they are leading young couples to Christ and helping them grow in their relationships with him. They have mobilized these couples to be involved in ministries across our city, from low-income Hispanic communities to the homeless downtown. Robert has also taken these young couples overseas, where he has equipped and empowered them to teach gospel-centered marriage principles to other couples in contexts around the world.

How about Holly? She is a young mom who recently left a comfortable suburban job to teach in an inner-city school. Holly doesn't just teach students, though; she invests in families with the gospel. She told me about one family she had recently visited— a single mom working full-time while going to school, with five children ages three to fifteen. This mom heats her house with their oven, and because furniture is not easy for her to come by, her children share single beds. Holly mobilized her small group to serve this family, and they are now in the process of bringing them beds and other supplies. Oh, and by the way, as I write this, Holly and her husband, John, are training church leaders in Sudan.

This is the picture. The plan of Christ is not dependent on having the right programs or hiring the right professionals but on building and being the right people—a community of people—who realize that we are all enabled and equipped to carry out the purpose of God for our lives. What happens when the Jims, Cathys, Roberts, and Hollys scattered all over the church begin taking ownership for accomplishing the plan of Christ? Soon they begin to realize that they were all indeed created to impact nations for his glory.

So how do we do it? If making disciples is the plan of Christ, and if it is accessible to all of us and expected of all of us, then how do we do it?

When you think about it, the fact that we lack a clear understanding about what it means to make disciples is astounding. This is the last command we have from Jesus to his followers before he left the earth. It is the central mission that Christ gave to his church before going to heaven. Yet if you were to ask individual Christians what it means to make disciples, you would likely get jumbled thoughts, ambiguous answers, and probably even some blank stares.

That's where I was—and to some extent still am. The more I read the Gospels, the more I marvel at the simple genius of what Jesus was doing with his disciples. My mind tends to wander toward grandiose dreams and intricate strategies, and I'm struck when I see Jesus simply, intentionally, systematically, patiently walking alongside twelve men. Jesus reminds me that disciples are not mass-produced. Disciples of Jesus—genuine, committed, self-sacrificing followers of Christ—are not made overnight.

Making disciples is not an easy process. It is trying. It is messy. It is slow, tedious, even painful at times. It is all these things because it is relational. Jesus has not given us an effortless step-by-step formula for impacting nations for his glory. He has given us people, and he has said, "Live for them. Love them, serve them, and lead them. Lead them to follow me, and lead them to lead others to follow me. In the process you will multiply the gospel to the ends of the earth."

To see what's involved in this, let's consider again those parting words of Jesus to his disciples—and to you and me. We are to *go* and make disciples of all nations. Then we are to *baptize* them in the name of the Father, Son, and Holy Spirit. And we are to *teach* them to obey everything Jesus commanded. All this adds up to the means to multiply people who enjoy God's grace and extend his glory around the world.

The Gospel and Bourbon Street

First, according to Jesus, disciple making involves going. It involves intentionally taking the gospel to people where they live, work, and play. Disciple making is not a call for others to come to us to hear the gospel but a command for us to go to others to share the gospel. A command for us to be gospel-living, gospel-speaking people at every moment and in every context where we find ourselves.

When my wife and I moved to New Orleans, I quickly found myself out of context. The city of New Orleans is unlike any other place, and the French Quarter is especially peculiar. Home to Bourbon Street, this part of the city has demographics that are diverse, to say the least. I remember the first time I walked through the heart of the Quarter. I noticed men and women from all walks of life going in and out of bars and restaurants. I saw wealthy couples out for a stroll walking by homeless men and women living on the streets. I observed what seemed to be a mixture of heterosexuals, homosexuals, bisexuals, and transvestites all within a few square blocks.

One of the most famous areas of the French Quarter is called Jackson Square. Nestled in front of a huge Roman Catholic cathedral, this park is always filled with people—locals and tourists alike. It is lined with street entertainers and tables manned by tarot card and palm readers, fortune-tellers and voodoo practitioners.

A couple of friends and I began to consider how we could communicate the gospel in the French Quarter. As we looked around at all the tables where people would sit down to have their palms read or fortunes told, we decided to get in on the action. So one day we set up a table of our own. Right next to the Voodoo Queen of New Orleans, we put out a table, covered it with a cloth and candles, positioned some chairs in front and behind, and propped up a sign that read "We'll Tell Your Future for Free."

People would come to the table and sit down with curious looks on their faces. "You'll tell me my future?"

"Guaranteed," we would say.

We were tempted to ask them to put out their palms, but we decided that was taking it too far. So we began by asking them a couple of simple questions. These questions were designed to establish the fact that they had sin in their lives so that we could look at them and say, "Your future does not look very good." Then we would begin sharing how their future could change because of Christ's work on the cross.

This ended up provoking some interesting dialogue, but it didn't take long for us to realize that sharing the gospel in the French Quarter was going to involve a lot of time and a load of work. For example, as we met homeless men and women, we quickly discovered that they were used to hearing the gospel or at least a version of it. It was common for them to have a tract put in their hands or to have condemnation rained down on them for their "sinful lifestyles." Most of the time the person telling them about the gospel disappeared the next minute.

When we first started talking about the gospel, people in the French Quarter figured we were just like all the others. So when we came back the next day and the next week and the week after that and the week after that, things started to change with them... and with us.

We started spending a lot of time in the Quarter. We would

take food with us when we could. We didn't have much money, and the cheapest food we could find was tacos from Burger King. Don't ask me why Burger King was selling tacos, but they were cheap, so we would grab a bag full of them and head down to the Quarter. These tacos (and the subsequent fried chicken we brought) provided an opportunity to sit on the streets of New Orleans and begin to build relationships. To hear about people's lives, their circumstances, their histories, their families, their dreams, and their struggles. And to share our own histories, families, dreams, and struggles with them.

One by one, homeless men and women began coming to faith in Christ. Before Hurricane Katrina hit, every Sunday morning as many as fifty of them would gather in the French Quarter for breakfast and worship. I recently went back to New Orleans and ran into one of the men from the Quarter who had trusted in Christ and had been baptized in the church. With tattoo-covered arms, he gave me a bear hug and said, "David, I want you to know that I'm now leading the homeless ministry in the French Quarter."

Disciple making is not about a program or an event but about a relationship. As we share the gospel, we impart life, and this is the essence of making disciples. Sharing the life of Christ.

This is why making disciples is not just about going, but it also includes baptizing.

WELCOME TO THE FAMILY

Baptism is the clear, public, symbolic picture of the new life we have in Christ. As illustrated in baptism, we have died with

Christ—died to our sin and died to ourselves—and we have been raised to life with him.[4]

Baptism also pictures our identification with one another in the church. Baptism unites us as brothers and sisters who share the life of Christ with one another.[5] Disciple making involves inviting people into a larger community of faith where they will see the life of Christ in action and experience the love of Christ in person.

Last week in our worship gathering we celebrated three baptisms. One person was a stay-at-home mom who had grown up in church and had lived a "good" life, but recently her eyes were opened for the first time to the reality of her sinfulness, even in her supposed goodness, and she trusted in Christ as her Savior and Lord. Another was a businessman who, after years of walking with Christ, realized that he had never been obedient to being baptized in identification with Christ and his church. The third was a former alcoholic, addict, and drug smuggler who had been radically saved by God's grace. (As a side note, recently he approached the guys in our church who lead overseas work to let them know he had skills conducive for smuggling contraband—in other words, Bibles—across borders. That is, if we were interested in using his expertise!)

As we celebrated the work of Christ in each of their lives, I praised God for the beauty of the body of Christ. Brought together from different backgrounds, and having journeyed through different struggles, we find ourselves joined together as one in the life of Christ. Disciple making involves identifying with a community of believers who show love to one another and share life with one another as we live together for the glory of God.

Earlier I mentioned Jim Shaddix, the seminary professor I went to New Orleans to study under. I am indebted to Jim for sharing his life with me in the same way Jesus did with his disciples. I gained much from sitting in classes that Jim taught, but even greater was the time we spent talking in his office, in his car on road trips, in his home with his family, and in the community as we shared the gospel.

I remember coming home one day after we had moved to New Orleans. I was in a hurry to change my clothes and leave our apartment. My wife asked what the rush was, and I told her that I was going running with Dr. Shaddix.

"Running?" she asked. "Since when are you a runner?"

"Since Dr. Shaddix asked me to run with him a couple of minutes ago," I replied.

I hate running. I have never been one of those guys who gets delight out of running in circles and going nowhere. But as soon as Dr. Shaddix asked me to join him on a run, I was a full-fledged cross-country athlete. You see, whether running in circles around the seminary campus or sitting in his home talking about life and ministry, Jim was gracious enough to share his life with me and in the process to show me what it means to follow Christ. And I wanted that, even if it included sweating.

Being a part of a community of faith involves being exposed to the life of Christ in others. Just as we are identified with Christ and his church in baptism, we now share life in Christ with one another. So to whom can you deliberately, intentionally, and sacrificially show the life of Christ in this way? This is foundational in making disciples, and we will multiply the gospel only when we allow others to get close enough to us to see the life of Christ in action.

RECEIVERS OR REPRODUCERS?

Going and baptizing are both crucial to disciple making. But they imply the need for something else just as crucial: teaching. This is an activity we all should take part in as we fulfill the life purpose God has given us. In our relationships with one another in the body of Christ, we are to be continually teaching one another the Word of Christ.

But when we hear Jesus talk about teaching, we need to be careful not to immediately jump in our minds to the classroom, lecture-style setting we often associate with teaching the Word. Classrooms and lectures have their place, but this is not the predominant kind of teaching we see in Jesus' relationship with his disciples. On the contrary, the world was a perpetual classroom for Jesus and his disciples, providing opportunities for instruction at every moment.

This is particularly important when we consider the command of Christ for each of us to make disciples. When we think about teaching, we often conclude that not everyone is intended to be a teacher. Scripture clearly speaks of a spiritual gift of teaching and identifies specific leadership roles in the church that are tied to the teaching of God's Word. Therefore, we assume that teaching is a task relegated to only a few. But while we should certainly acknowledge and affirm gifted teachers given by God to the church, Jesus' command for us to make disciples envisions a teaching role for all of us.

For example, imagine "going" and leading someone to faith in Christ and then seeing her "baptized" in identification with Christ and his church. Now what? How is she going to learn to walk with Christ daily? If teaching is limited to a select few in the church who are equipped for that, then we will immediately tell this new Christian she needs to sit in a classroom and learn from a teacher. Thus we get the common approach to "discipleship" today—a far cry from the disciple making of Jesus. It's not that sitting in lecture-style settings is not beneficial, but what if Christ has actually set *us* up to be the teachers?

Think about it. What would be the most effective way for this new follower of Christ to learn to pray? To sign her up for a one-hour-a-week class on prayer? Or to invite her personally into your quiet time with God to teach her how to pray?

Similarly, what would be the most effective way for this new follower of Christ to learn to study the Bible? To register her in the next available course on Bible study? Or to sit down with her and walk her through the steps of how you have learned to study the Bible?

This raises the bar in our own Christianity. In order to teach someone else how to pray, we need to know how to pray. In order to help someone else learn how to study the Bible, we need to be active in studying the Bible. But this is the beauty of making disciples. When we take responsibility for helping others grow in

Christ, it automatically takes our own relationship with Christ to a new level.

Take Matt, for example. He came to me asking all kinds of questions about how to share the gospel with a group of Mormons he works with. He didn't know where to start. I recommended some resources, and Matt started researching Mormonism and all the differences between the gospel and Mormon teachings. In the process he started sharing Christ with Mormon co-workers. A few weeks later Matt sent me an e-mail in which he said, "Because of this study and being able to share the gospel, my strength and faith in Christ are stronger and more confirmed than ever. My wife has already noticed a difference in my own personal walk with Christ, and I am praising God for giving me this opportunity."

When faced with the prospect of sharing the gospel with people whose beliefs he did not understand, Matt could have said, "I'm not equipped to do this; someone else will have to do it." Instead Matt took responsibility for teaching the Word of Christ himself, and he began to grow in his walk with Christ in ways he never would have otherwise.

I often ask members of our church if they are receivers or reproducers of God's Word. Let me illustrate the difference.

Imagine being in Sudan. You walk into a thatched hut with a small group of Sudanese church leaders, and you sit down to teach them God's Word. As soon as you start, you lose eye contact with all of them. No one is looking at you, and you hardly see their eyes the rest of the time. The reason is because they're writing down every word you say. They come up to you afterward and say, "Teacher, we are going to take everything we have learned from God's Word, translate it into our languages, and teach it in our tribes." They were not listening to receive but to reproduce.

Now journey with me to a contemporary worship service in the United States. Some people have their Bibles open, while others don't have a Bible with them. A few people are taking notes, but for the most part they are passively sitting in the audience. While some are probably disengaged, others are intently focused on what the preacher is saying, listening to God's Word to hear how it applies to their lives. But the reality is, few are listening to reproduce.

We are, by nature, receivers. Even if we have a desire to learn God's Word, we still listen from a default self-centered mind-set that is always asking, *What can I get out of this?* But as we have seen, this is unbiblical Christianity. What if we changed the question whenever we gathered to learn God's Word? What if we began to think, *How can I listen to his Word so that I am equipped to teach this Word to others?*

This changes everything. All of a sudden the pen and the paper come out. Note taking is not the measure of how committed we are to making disciples, but if we are hearing God's Word taught in order to teach others, then we want to get it down as best we can. When we realize we have the responsibility to teach the Word, it changes everything about how we hear the Word.

It also changes who hears the Word. Now the Word that is being preached in a worship gathering or taught in a small-group setting is subsequently being translated into contexts and spheres of influence represented all across a church. God's Word is no longer just being heard in a building; it is being multiplied throughout a community. It is multiplying because the people of God are no longer listening as if his Word is intended to stop with them. They are now living as if God's Word is intended to spread through them.

This is exhilarating for me as a pastor. When I or someone else in our church teaches God's Word on a Sunday morning, I know that his truth is not confined in that building. That same truth will be taught in a women's shelter later that night. It will be taught in workplace Bible studies throughout that week. It will be taught the next weekend in the Birmingham city jail and in a nearby drug rehabilitation facility. In the days to come, it will be translated and taught by our people to pastors in Latin America and new Christ followers in Central Asia. Exciting things happen when the people of God believe the Word of God is worth spending their lives to teach to others.

DISCIPLING OR DISINFECTING?

Making disciples by going, baptizing, and teaching people the Word of Christ and then enabling them to do the same thing in other people's lives—this is the plan God has for each of us to impact nations for the glory of Christ.

This plan seems so counterintuitive to our way of thinking. In a culture where bigger is always better and flashy is always more effective, Jesus beckons each of us to plainly, humbly, and quietly focus our lives on people. The reality is, you can't share life like this with masses and multitudes. Jesus didn't. He spent three years with twelve guys. If the Son of God thought it necessary to focus his life on a small group of men, we are fooling ourselves to think we can mass-produce disciples today. God's design for taking the gospel to the world is a slow, intentional, simple process that involves every one of his people sacrificing every facet of their lives to multiply the life of Christ in others.

I was in Cuba a few weeks ago, and this is exactly the picture I saw. In Cuba you will not observe large church buildings and flashy church advertisements. You will hardly notice the church at all…until you get to know the people. We visited one small, impoverished Cuban church. This one church had planted sixty other churches. The next day we visited one of the churches they had planted. That church had planted twenty-five other churches. Cuban Christians are taking Jesus at his word and multiplying the church by making disciples. Nothing big and nothing extravagant. Just going, baptizing, and teaching, and in the process planting churches from coast to coast across that island nation.

But we resist this plan, resorting to performances and programs that seem much more "successful." In our Christian version of the American dream, our plan ends up disinfecting Christians from the world more than discipling Christians in the world. Let me explain the difference.

Disinfecting Christians from the world involves isolating followers of Christ in a spiritual safe-deposit box called the church building and teaching them to be good. In this strategy, success in the church is defined by how big a building you have to house all the Christians, and the goal is to gather as many people as possible for a couple of hours each week in that place where we are isolated and insulated from the realities of the world around us. When someone asks, "Where is your church?" we point them to a building or give them an address, and everything centers around what happens at that location.

When we gather at the building, we learn to be good. Being good is defined by what we avoid in the world. We are holy because of what we don't participate in (and at this point we may be the only organization in the world defining success by what we don't do). We live decent lives in decent homes with decent jobs and decent families as decent citizens. We are decent church members with little more impact on the world than we had before we were saved. Though thousands may join us, ultimately we have turned a deaf ear to billions who haven't even heard his name.

Discipling is much different.

Whereas disinfecting Christians involves isolating them and teaching them to be good, discipling Christians involves propelling Christians into the world to risk their lives for the sake of others. Now the world is our focus, and we gauge success in the church not on the hundreds or thousands whom we can get into our buildings but on the hundreds or thousands who are leaving our buildings to take on the world with the disciples they are making. In this case, we would never think that the disciple-making plan of Jesus could take place in one service a week at one location led by one or two teachers. Disciple making takes place multiple times every week in multiple locations by an army of men and women sharing, showing, and teaching the Word of Christ and together serving a world in need of Christ.

All of a sudden, holiness is defined by what we do. We are now a community of faith taking Jesus at his word and following his plan, even when it does not make sense to the culture around us and even when it costs us.

In the process we are realizing that we actually were intended to reach the world for the glory of Christ, and we are discovering that the purpose for which we were created is accessible to every one of us. Children and the elderly, students and workers, men and women all joined together in a body that is united with other followers of Christ around the world in a practical strategy to make disciples and impact nations for the glory of Christ. A community of Christians each multiplying the gospel by going, baptizing, and teaching in the contexts where they live every day. Is anything else, according to the Bible, even considered a church?

CHAPTER SIX

How Much
Is Enough?

AMERICAN WEALTH AND
A WORLD OF POVERTY

We all have blind spots—areas of our lives that need to be uncovered so we can see correctly and adjust our lives accordingly. But they are hard to identify. Others can often see them in us, and we rely on friends to point them out. But the reality is, even then we have a hard time recognizing them. We don't want to admit they exist…often until it's too late. We discover them in hindsight, but we struggle to see them in the present.

I can think of at least one glaring blind spot in American Christian history. Slavery. How could Christians who supposedly believed the gospel so easily rationalize the enslavement of other human beings? Churchgoers with good intentions worshiping God together every Sunday and reading the Bible religiously all week long, all the while using God's Word to justify treating men, women, and children as property to be used or abused. They actually thought they were generous when they gave their slaves an extra chicken at Christmas.

This frightens me. Good intentions, regular worship, and even study of the Bible do not prevent blindness in us. Part of our sinful nature instinctively chooses to see what we want to see and to ignore what we want to ignore. I can live my Christian life and even lead the church while unknowingly overlooking evil.

Not long ago God began uncovering a blind spot in my life. An area of disobedience. A reality in God's Word that I had pretended did not exist. More aptly put, I had lived as if it did not exist. But God brought me to a place of confession before him, before my family, and before the faith family I lead.

Today more than a billion people in the world live and die in desperate poverty. They attempt to survive on less than a dollar per day. Close to two billion others live on less than two dollars per day. That's nearly half the world struggling today to find food, water, and shelter with the same amount of money I spend on french fries for lunch.

More than twenty-six thousand children today will breathe their last breath due to starvation or a preventable disease. To put it in perspective for me, that's twenty-six thousand Joshuas and Calebs (my two sons). To put it in perspective for the church I pastor, if this were happening among the children in my community, then every child eighteen years or younger in our county would be dead within the next two days.

Suddenly I began to realize that if I have been commanded to make disciples of all nations, and if poverty is rampant in the world to which God has called me, then I cannot ignore these realities. Anyone wanting to proclaim the glory of Christ to the ends of the earth must consider not only how to declare the gospel verbally but also how to demonstrate the gospel visibly in a world where so many are urgently hungry. If I am going to address urgent spiritual need by sharing the gospel of Christ or building up the body of Christ around the world, then I cannot overlook dire physical need in the process.

Frighteningly, though, I have turned a blind eye to these realities. I have practically ignored these people, and I have been successful in my ignorance because they are not only poor but also powerless. Literally millions of them are dying in obscurity, and I have enjoyed my affluence while pretending they don't exist.

But they *do* exist. Not only do they exist, but God takes very seriously how I respond to them. The book of Proverbs warns about curses that come upon those who ignore the poor. The prophets warn of God's judgment and devastation for those who neglect the poor. Jesus pronounces woes upon the wealthy who trust in their riches, and James tells those who hoard their money and live in self-indulgence to "weep and wail because of the misery that is coming" upon them.[1] In a humbling passage, Jesus says to those who turn away from him by ignoring the physical needs of his people, "Depart from me, you who are cursed, into the eternal fire prepared for the devil and his angels."[2]

Now, I immediately want to guard against a potentially serious misunderstanding in this chapter. The Bible nowhere teaches that caring for the poor is a means by which we earn salvation. The means of our salvation is faith in Christ alone, and the basis of our salvation is the work of Christ alone. We are not saved by caring for the poor, and one of the worst possible responses to this chapter would be to strive to care for the poor in order to earn salvation or standing before God.

Yet, while caring for the poor is not the basis of our salvation, this does not mean that our use of wealth is totally disconnected from our salvation. Indeed, caring for the poor (among other things) is *evidence* of our salvation. The faith in Christ that saves us from our sins involves an internal transformation that has external implications. According to Jesus, you can tell someone is a follower of Christ by the fruit of his or her life, and the writers of the New Testament show us that the fruit of faith in Christ involves material concern for the poor.[3] Caring for the poor is one natural overflow and a necessary evidence of the presence of Christ in our hearts. If there is no sign of caring for the poor in our lives, then there is reason to at least question whether Christ is in our hearts.[4]

Some might think this is taking things too far, but consider another scenario. Imagine a man who claims to have Christ in his heart but indulges in sexual activity with multiple partners every week. When he is confronted by Scripture about his sin, he nevertheless continues in willful sexual immorality. He disobeys Christ persistently with no sign of remorse, contrition, or conviction. So is he really a Christian?

Of course, we are not this man's ultimate judge. But when we look at 1 Corinthians 6:9–10 and it says, "Neither the sexually immoral…nor adulterers…will inherit the kingdom of God," we would certainly question whether this man is really a child of God. It is not that he needs to stop his sexual immorality to be saved.

That would mean he would need to earn his salvation. No, he needs to trust in Christ, which will result in a changed heart with a desire to obey Christ in this area of his life.

So what is the difference between someone who willfully indulges in sexual pleasures while ignoring the Bible on moral purity and someone who willfully indulges in the selfish pursuit of more and more material possessions while ignoring the Bible on caring for the poor? The difference is that one involves a social taboo in the church and the other involves the social norm in the church.[5]

We look back on slave-owning churchgoers of 150 years ago and ask, "How could they have treated their fellow human beings that way?" I wonder if followers of Christ 150 years from now will look back at Christians in America today and ask, "How could they live in such big houses? How could they drive such nice cars and wear such nice clothes? How could they live in such affluence while thousands of children were dying because they didn't have food and water? How could they go on with their lives as though the billions of poor didn't even exist?"

Is materialism a blind spot in American Christianity today? More specifically, is materialism a blind spot in *your* Christianity today? Surely this is something we must uncover, for if our lives do not reflect radical compassion for the poor, there is reason to question just how effective we will be in declaring the glory of Christ to the ends of the earth. More pointedly, if our lives do not reflect radical compassion for the poor, there is reason to wonder if Christ is really in us at all.

Necessary Clarifications

Before we explore this blind spot more fully, a couple of qualifying points:

First, I am a pastor, not an economist. I am deeply grateful for men and women in the church I pastor and elsewhere who are far wiser than I am in fiscal matters. While I have had intensive discussions with many of them and have researched issues ranging from individual and corporate finances to economic and social structures, the last thing I presume to be is an expert. Nevertheless, as a pastor I need to pose some questions regarding the use of our money that I believe the gospel requires us to ask.

Second, my purpose in this chapter is not to provide an overview of everything the Bible teaches about money and possessions. Of course, important principles are expressed throughout Scripture on the subject. One such principle is that wealth is not inherently evil. Scripture does not condemn riches or possessions in and of themselves. In fact, Scripture teaches that God gives us material resources for our good. In the words of Paul, God "richly provides us with everything for our enjoyment."[6] Much error would occur if someone walked away from this chapter thinking that money and possessions are necessarily bad; they are actually good gifts from the hand of God intended for our enjoyment and the spread of his glory.

Since other Bible truths about money and possessions are not fully addressed in this chapter, I have provided an extensive resource of teachings, articles, books, and links regarding a biblical theology of possessions to help place what I do address here in a larger context. These can be found on the Web site that accompanies this book (www.radicalthebook.com). I encourage you to make use of them.

In summary, the purpose of this chapter is simple. My goal is to share with you how God has been opening my eyes to a major blind spot in my life and in the church I lead. In the process I challenge you to consider if it is a blind spot in your life. If it is, then I want to dare you to look across the landscape of starving millions through the eyes of Christ, who "though he was rich, yet for your sakes he became poor, so that you through his poverty might become rich."[7] And as you do, I challenge you to let the gospel radically transform the way you understand and use your possessions in our American culture.

THE RICH MAN

So is caring for the poor a serious matter to God?

Listen to the story Jesus told one day to a group of religious leaders who loved money and justified their indulgences because of the culture around them. He told them about a rich man who lived in luxury while he ignored a poor man, Lazarus, who sat outside his gate, covered with sores and surrounded by dogs, eating the scraps that fell from the rich man's table.

As we read in Luke 16, the day came when both men died. The rich man went to hell, and the poor man went to heaven. The rich man could see into heaven, and he cried out for relief from the agony of hell. The reply from heaven came. "Son, remember that in your lifetime you received your good things, while Lazarus received bad things, but now he is comforted here, and you are in agony. And besides all this, between us and you a great chasm has been fixed, so that those who want to go from here to you cannot, nor can anyone cross over from there to us."[8]

This story illustrates God's response to the needs of the poor. The poor man's name, Lazarus, literally means "God is my help." Sick, crippled, and impoverished, Lazarus received compassion from God. Of course, just because someone is poor does not make him righteous before God and therefore fit for heaven. At the same time, though, a quick perusal through Scripture shows that God hears, feeds, satisfies, rescues, defends, raises up, and secures justice for the poor who trust in him.[9]

But this story also illustrates God's response to those who neglect the poor. He responds to them with condemnation. Again, the Bible does not teach that wealth alone implies unrighteousness or warrants condemnation. The rich man in this story is not in hell because he had money. Instead, he is in hell because he lacked faith in God, leading him to indulge in luxuries while ignoring the poor outside his gate.[10] As a result, earth was his heaven, and eternity became his hell.

Now I have to ask the question. When you hear this story from Jesus' mouth, with whom do you identify more—Lazarus or the rich man? For that matter, with whom do *I* identify more?

In uncovering this blind spot in my life, God has made it clear that I look a lot like the rich man in this story. I don't always think of myself as rich, and I'm guessing you may not think of yourself as rich either. But the reality is, if you and I have running water, shelter over our heads, clothes to wear, food to eat, and some means of transportation (even if it's public transportation), then we are in the top 15 percent of the world's people for wealth.

I am much like the rich man, and the church I lead looks a lot like him too. Every Sunday we gather in a multimillion-dollar building with millions of dollars in vehicles parked outside. We leave worship to spend thousands of dollars on lunch before returning to hundreds of millions of dollars' worth of homes. We live in luxury.

Meanwhile, the poor man is outside our gate. And he is hungry. In the time we gather for worship on a Sunday morning, almost a thousand children elsewhere die because they have no food. If it were our kids starving, they would all be gone by the time we said our closing prayer. We certainly wouldn't ignore our kids while we sang songs and entertained ourselves, but we are content with ignoring other parents' kids. Many of them are our spiritual brothers and sisters in developing nations. They are suffering from malnutrition, deformed bodies and brains, and preventable diseases. At most, we are throwing our scraps to them while we indulge in our pleasures here. Kind of like an extra chicken for the slaves at Christmas.

This is not what the people of God do. Regardless of what we say or sing or study on Sunday morning, rich people who neglect the poor are not the people of God.[11]

WHAT ARE WE BUILDING?

What scares me most, though, is that we can pretend that we are the people of God. We can comfortably turn a blind eye to these words in the Bible and go on with our affluent model of Christianity and church. We can even be successful in our church culture for doing so. It will actually be a sign of success and growth when we spend millions on ourselves. "Look how big that church is becoming," they'll say. "Did you see all the stuff they have?"

I think we actually believe that what we're doing is biblical. And so did Jesus' disciples. That's one of the reasons they were so shocked when Jesus walked away from his conversation with a rich young man, saying, "How hard it is for the rich to enter the kingdom of God!" The very next verse says, "The disciples were amazed at his words."[12] Why were they so surprised?

The answer is steeped in Old Testament history. From the beginning of the nation of Israel, God had promised to bless them materially. God poured out material blessings on Abraham, Isaac, Jacob, and Joseph. God promised his people that as they obeyed him, they would receive abundant material prosperity.[13]

Why the promise of material possessions? God was forming a nation for himself that would be a demonstration of his greatness to all other nations. In so doing, God established a place for his people and his glory to dwell. David and Solomon amassed great amounts of wealth as they established a kingdom, and one important part of that kingdom was the temple that Solomon would build. As seen in 1 Kings 8, Solomon dedicated the temple and asked God to make his glory known through his people in that place.[14] Material blessing aimed toward the establishment of the people of God in a physical place with a physical temple is a fundamental part of the history of Israel.

So when a rich Jewish man came up to Jesus, and Jesus told

him, "Go, sell everything you have and give to the poor," the disciples were naturally confused.[15] *Why would obedience to Christ lead to this man losing his possessions?*

The disciples would soon realize that a radical shift was taking place. It was not that God had changed or that the God of the Old Testament was somehow different from the God of the New Testament. Instead, the eternal plan of God was unfolding, and Jesus was ushering in a new phase in redemptive history, one that would affect the relationship between faith and material blessing.

In the dawn of this new phase in redemptive history, no teachers (including Jesus) in the New Testament ever promise material wealth as a reward for obedience.[16] As if this were not startling enough to first-century Jews (and twenty-first-century American Christians), we also see no verse in the New Testament where God's people are ever again commanded to build a majestic place of worship. Instead God's people are told to be the temple—the place of worship.[17] And their possessions are to be spent on building, not a place where people can come to see God's glory, but a people who are taking God's glory to the world.

All this begs the question, have we taken this shift in redemptive history into account in the way we approach our possessions today?

Isn't the hidden assumption among many Christians in our culture that if we follow God, things will go well for us materially? Such thinking is explicit in "health and wealth" teaching, and it is implicit in the lives of Christians whose use of possessions looks virtually the same as that of our non-Christian neighbors.

One evening I was meeting with an underground house

church overseas, and we were discussing various issues in Scripture. A woman who lived in the city and knew some English shared. "I have a television, and every once in a while I am able to get stations from the United States," she said. "Some of these stations have church services on them. I see the preachers, and they are dressed in very nice clothes, and they are preaching in very nice buildings. Some of them even tell me that if I have faith, I too can have nice things."

She paused before continuing. "When I come to our church meetings, I look around, and most of us are very poor, and we are meeting here at great risk to our lives." Then she looked at me and asked, "Does this mean we do not have enough faith?"

In that moment I realized the extent to which we, as churches and Christians across America, are in some cases explicitly and in other cases implicitly exporting a theology that equates faith in Christ with prosperity in this world. This is fundamentally *not* the radical picture of Christianity we see in the New Testament.

Further, when we pool our resources in our churches, what are our priorities? Every year in the United States, we spend more than $10 billion on church buildings. In America alone, the amount of real estate owned by institutional churches is worth over $230 billion. We have money and possessions, and we are building temples everywhere. Empires, really. Kingdoms. We call them houses of worship. But at the core, aren't they too often outdated models of religion that wrongfully define worship according to a place and wastefully consume our time and money when God has called us to be a people who spend our lives for the sake of his glory among the needy outside our gates?

My heart aches even as I write this, because the reality is that I preach every Sunday in one of these giant buildings. How do we even begin to reverse the trends regarding where we spend our resources? I constantly wrestle with this question, and I don't believe it's a question for just pastors and church building committees. Like the rich young man in Mark 10, every Christian has to wrestle with what Jesus is calling us to do with our resources as we follow him.

SELL EVERYTHING YOU HAVE?

Well, are we really supposed to abandon our possessions? Isn't that a bit extreme? Let's journey back to Jesus' conversation with the rich young man in Mark 10 and see if it is.

This man eagerly approached Jesus and asked him one simple, all-important question: "What must I do to inherit eternal life?" Jesus eventually said to him, "One thing you lack. Go, sell everything you have and give to the poor, and you will have treasure in heaven. Then come, follow me."[18]

Jesus was clearly exposing this man's allegiance to his possessions. Following Jesus would involve total trust in him, an abandonment of everything the man owned. Fundamentally, the rich man needed a new heart, one that was radically transformed by the gospel.[19]

I think there are two common errors people make when they read this passage.

First, some try to universalize Jesus' words, saying that he *always* commands his followers to sell everything they have and give it to the poor. But the New Testament doesn't support this. Even some of the disciples, who admittedly abandoned much to follow Christ, still had a home, likely still had a boat, and probably had some kind of material support. So, obviously, following Jesus doesn't necessarily imply a loss of all your private property and possessions.

This causes many of us to breathe a sigh of relief. But before we sigh too deeply, we need to see the other error in interpreting Mark 10, which is to assume that Jesus *never* calls his followers to abandon all their possessions to follow him. If Mark 10 teaches anything, it teaches us that Jesus does sometimes call people to sell everything they have and give it to the poor.[20] This means he might call you or me to do this. I love the way one writer put it. He wrote, "That Jesus did not command all his followers to sell all their possessions gives comfort only to the kind of people to whom he *would* issue that command."[21]

So what about you and me? Are we willing to ask God if he wants us to sell everything we have and give the money to the poor? Are we willing to ask and wait for an answer instead of providing one of our own or justifying our ideas of why he would never tell us to do this? This seems a bit radical, but isn't it normal and expected when we follow a Master who said, "Any of you who does not give up everything he has cannot be my disciple"?[22]

Once again we find ourselves back at what it means to follow the Jesus of the Bible, not the Jesus we have created and are comfortable with. The rich man in Mark 10 didn't see Jesus for who he was. The rich man perceived him as a respectable religious figure, calling him "good teacher."[23] However, Jesus was not, and never is, interested in being seen as a respectable teacher. He is the sovereign Lord. He doesn't give options for people to consider; he gives commands for people to obey.

So, then, what if he told you and me to sell everything we have? What if he told us to sell our houses for simpler living arrangements? What if he told us to sell our cars for more modest ones—or for no cars at all? What if he told us to give away all but a couple of sets of clothes? What if he told us to empty the savings account we have been building for years if not decades? What if he told us to change our lifestyles completely?

Now, before you and I think of all the reasons he would not tell us to do these things, we need to think about this question first: is he Lord?

Are you and I looking to Jesus for advice that seems fiscally responsible according to the standards of the world around us? Or are we looking to Jesus for total leadership in our lives, even if that means going against everything our affluent culture and maybe even our affluent religious neighbors might tell us to do?

Jesus never intended to be one voice among many counseling us on how to lead our lives and use our money. He always intends to be *the* voice that guides whatever decisions we make in our lives and with our money.

TRUTH IN LOVE

Possibilities such as the ones we are considering will make many of us uneasy, but this is what I appreciate most about Jesus' conversation with the rich man. Jesus obviously gave him a tough command to follow, and it seems cold, if not extreme, when it comes out of his mouth. He was going right for the jugular, so to speak, with a guy who had great wealth. Jesus was launching a direct attack on the sense of security and stability this man had in this world.

Words like these can seem hard to us too. When Jesus calls you or me to let go of things, to sacrifice things, to sell things, to give away things, it's not easy. What will we do? Where will we live? What if something unexpected happens in the future? Our sense of security and stability is immediately threatened when we think about truly letting Jesus reign over our possessions.

But the beauty of this conversation is what the Bible tells us in Mark 10:21: "Jesus looked at him and loved him." What a wonderful phrase! Jesus was not telling this man to give away everything he had because Jesus hated him or desired to make his life miserable. Jesus was telling him to give away everything he had because Jesus *loved* him.

Jesus apparently loves rich people enough to tell them the truth.

Luke 12 echoes this theme of love. There we read how Jesus told all his disciples, "Sell your possessions and give to the poor." But listen to what he said right before that: "Do not be afraid, little flock, for your Father has been pleased to give you the kingdom."[24]

The imagery in this simple verse is diverse and breathtaking. In God we have a Shepherd who protects us from fear as if we're a little flock. In God we have a Father who delights in us as children, a Father who is determined to give good gifts to us. And in God we have a King who guarantees a kingdom for us.

Let me amplify and paraphrase, then, what it seems Jesus was saying: "In light of the fact that you have a God in heaven who is set on caring for you as a shepherd does his sheep, as a father does his children, and as a king does who is passing on an entire kingdom, don't be anxious. Sell your possessions, give to the poor, and don't worry. Your God—your Shepherd, your Father, your King—has everything under control."

A wealthier man in our faith family came to my office after we had been studying the story of the rich young man. He sat down, looked at me, and said point-blank, "I think you're crazy for saying some of the things you are saying." Then he paused, and I wasn't sure what direction this conversation was going to go. He continued, "But I think you're right. And so now I think I'm crazy for thinking some of the things I'm thinking."

For the next few minutes, he described how he was selling his large house and had decided to give away many of his other possessions. He talked about the needs he wanted to invest his resources in for the glory of Christ. Then he looked at me through tears in his eyes and said, "I wonder at some points if I'm being irresponsible or unwise. But then I realize there is never going to come a day when I stand before God and he looks at me and says, 'I wish you would have kept more for yourself.' I'm confident that God will take care of me."

When God tells us to give extravagantly, we can trust him to do the same in our lives. And this is really the core issue of it all. Do we trust him? Do we trust Jesus when he tells us to give radically for the sake of the poor? Do we trust him to provide for us when we begin using the resources he has given us to provide for others? Do we trust him to know what is best for our lives, our families, and our financial futures?

It's Hard for a Rich Man

To be honest, as strong as God's Word is with these promises, my wife and I have struggled with this. When God began uncovering this blind spot in our lives, we had a hard time really saying, "God, we will sell, give away, and change anything and everything you want." We liked our house, not just because it was where we lived, but because it represented stability and security, and it was a sanctuary of sorts for our family. We liked our lifestyle. It was convenient and comfortable for us and for our kids. As we began putting each of our possessions and all our finances on the table, we began to discover the hold many of them had on our lives.

We saw the gruesome reality of 1 Timothy 6 playing out in our hearts: "People who want to get rich fall into temptation and a trap and into many foolish and harmful desires that plunge men into ruin and destruction."[25] Paul is talking here about simply the *desire* to be rich. So how much more does it apply to those who actually *are* rich? Our possessions can be deadly. They can be subtly deadly.

That's why Jesus said it's hard for a rich man to enter the kingdom of God. Ultimately, Jesus was communicating to this man that there was nothing he could do to enter the kingdom of God apart from total trust in God. It is impossible for us to earn our way into heaven. In the process, though, Jesus was exposing the barrier that this man's wealth was to seeing his need for God. His wealth on earth would ultimately keep him from eternal treasure.

The reality is, most of us in our culture and in the American church simply don't believe Jesus or Paul on this one. We just don't believe that our wealth can be a barrier to entering the kingdom of God. We are fine with thinking of affluence, comfort, and material possessions as blessings. But they cannot be barriers. We think the way the world thinks—that wealth is always to our advantage. But Jesus is saying the exact opposite. He is saying that wealth can be a dangerous obstacle.

That's why Paul says in 1 Timothy 6:6, "Godliness with contentment is great gain." In the context of this passage, contentment is described as having food and clothing, having the necessities of life provided for. Put this together with verse 9 (which we saw earlier), and those who desire to be rich and acquire more than the necessities of life are in danger of being plunged into ruin and destruction.

This passage begs the question, am I willing to live a life that is content with food and clothing, having the basic necessities of my life provided for? Or do I want more? Do I want a bigger house or a nicer car or better clothes? Do I want to indulge in more and more luxuries in my life? After all, what's wrong with luxuries?

This is a key question, and if we are not careful in how we answer it, we will miss the point of what God desires to teach us about our possessions. We don't need to sell or give away nice clothes, nice cars, nice houses, or surplus possessions because they are inherently bad. As we have seen, wealth and possessions are not inherently evil; they are good in and of themselves. So we don't sell them or give them away because they are sinful.

Then why do we sell them or give them away? We sell them and give them away because Christ in us compels us to care for the needy around us.

John Wesley (1703–91) provides us with an example of how to see our possessions in light of needs around us. Listen to this story about a purchase Wesley once made for his apartment:

> [Wesley] had just finished buying some pictures for his room when one of the chambermaids came to his door. It was a Winter day and he noticed that she had only a thin linen gown to wear for protection against the cold. He reached into his pocket to give her some money for a coat, and found he had little left. It struck him that the Lord was not pleased with how he had spent his money. He asked himself: "Will Thy Master say, 'Well done, good and faithful steward?' Thou hast adorned thy walls with the money that might have screened this poor creature from the cold! O justice! O mercy! Are not these pictures the blood of this poor maid?"[26]

Were the pictures that Wesley had hanging in his room wrong in and of themselves? Absolutely not. But it was wrong—very wrong—to buy unnecessary decoration for himself when a woman was freezing outside without a coat.

Now, we need to be careful not to misconstrue this illustration. The point is not that every picture on the wall in your house or my house is evil. (For the record, there are pictures on the wall in my house!) The point is also not that we need to feel guilty whenever we purchase anything that is not an absolute necessity. The reality is that most everything in our lives in the American culture would be classified as a luxury, not a necessity. The computer I am writing this book on, the spoon and fork I will eat my dinner with later this evening, and the bed and pillow I will sleep on tonight (in addition to many other things in my life) are all luxuries. The point we can learn from this event in Wesley's life is that our perspective on our possessions radically changes when we open our eyes to the needs of the world around us. When we have the courage to look in the faces of brothers and sisters whose bodies are malnourished and whose brains are deformed because they have no food, Christ will change our desires, and we will long to sacrifice our resources for the glory of his name among them.

So what would happen if we uncovered this blind spot in our lives and began paying attention to those who are in need? What if we took a serious look at them and actually began to adjust our lifestyles for the sake of the gospel among them? What would that look like? Think about the possibilities.

As I mentioned, little of what we have would be considered necessities, and as long as we are living in our culture, we will be surrounded by luxuries. So why not simply begin a process of limiting and eliminating some of them? Why not begin selling and giving away luxuries for the sake of the poor outside our gates? Why not begin operating under the idea that God has given us excess, not so we could *have* more, but so we could *give* more?

Now we're getting radical.

Or maybe we're getting biblical.[27]

Let's dare to take things a step further. What if we actually set a cap on our lifestyles? What if we got to the point where we could draw a line, saying, "This is enough, and I am giving away everything I have or earn above this line"?

This is what Wesley did. He identified a modest level of expenses that he was going to live on every year. The first year his income surpassed that level by a small amount, and he gave that excess away. The next year his income increased, but he kept his standard of living the same, so he had more to give away. This continued year after year. At one point Wesley was making the equivalent of about $160,000 a year in today's terms, but he was living as if he were making $20,000 a year. As a result, he had the equivalent of more than $140,000 to give away that year.

Consider what could happen. What if you and I decided that having a $50,000 salary doesn't necessitate living a $50,000 lifestyle? What if you and I had simple caps on our lifestyles and were free to give the rest of our resources away for the glory of Christ in the neediest parts of the world?

Scripture clearly teaches that God intends our plenty to supply others' needs.[28] In John Calvin's commentary on 2 Corinthians 8–9, he noted that God "has enjoined upon us frugality and temperance, and has forbidden, that any one should go to excess, taking advantage of his abundance. Let those, then, that have riches…consider that their abundance was not intended to be laid out in intemperance or excess, but in relieving the necessities of the brethren."[29] As the practical outworking of this truth, Calvin once said that half of the church's funds should be allotted specifically for the poor (a far cry from most church budgets today).[30] While he did not expect everyone to enjoy the same resources, Calvin concluded that "no one is to be allowed to starve."[31]

"What Can We Spare?" or "What Will It Take?"

We are tempted, though, to settle for throwing our scraps to the poor. For this reason I am indebted to a good friend who helped me evaluate what I am willing to give away. Jason lives with his family in a country where it's illegal to spread the gospel. He is serving people there who have never heard of Jesus. He once wrote me with reference to the millions of people who still have not heard the gospel:

> How many people have not believed because they have not heard? What will it take for those people to hear? Have they not heard because there is no one to tell them? What can we do, in obedience to God, to change a world in which there are millions and millions of people who cannot call on the name of the Lord? Most of us would say we know the answer to that question. Many of us would say we are even doing things to change the situation. But the truth is, there will continue to be millions and millions of people who do not hear as long as we continue to use spare time and spare money to reach them. Those are two radically different questions. "What can we spare?" and "What will it take?"

His final two questions challenged me to the core, not only as they pertained to reaching the unreached, but also as they related to caring for the poor. *What would happen,* I thought, *if we stopped asking how much we could spare and started asking how much it was going to take?*

Now, I am not assuming that you and I can single-handedly give enough to alleviate poverty. Poverty, after all, is rooted in social, political, economic, moral, material, and many other factors. Some we can affect (even if in small ways), and others are beyond our influence. Clearly, God does not command or expect us to meet every need. But the logic that says, "I can't do everything, so I won't do anything," is straight from hell.

What would happen if together we stopped giving our scraps to the poor and started giving surplus? What if we started giving not just what we are able to give but beyond what we are able to give? What if, like the widow in Luke 21 who gave all she had, we began to give what it hurt us to give? What if we gave like this, not just because of the critical need around us, but because this kind of giving is actually what the heart of Christ in us both demands and desires?

Free to Give

And this is exactly what Scripture teaches. In 1 Timothy 6, Paul tells Timothy to command the rich "to do good, to be rich in good deeds, and to be generous and willing to share."[32] This, Paul says, is the key to being free from the deadly nature of wealth and possessions. Give. Give generously, abundantly, and sacrificially. Give not because your stuff is bad. Give because Christ is in you. Give because your heart has been captured by a Savior who has produced in you "overflowing joy," welling up in "rich generosity."[33]

This is the kind of freedom the disciples were familiar with. After Jesus' conversation with the rich young man, Peter turned to Jesus and exclaimed, "We have left everything to follow you!"[34] In great contrast to the rich man who walked away from Jesus feeling sad, here was a disciple free from slavery to money and stuff, free from earthly security and worldly comforts.

I have seen that freedom in the faith family I lead. After one Sunday in our church when we were studying the story of the rich young man in Mark 10, I received the following e-mail from one of our members:

> My wife and I went home, emptied all our clothes onto the bed, got several bags of canned goods and all the baby clothes our son has grown out of in addition to the toys he doesn't play with anymore. I took several hundred dollars cash that I was saving to upgrade the front lawn and drove over to the projects downtown and prayed. I prayed for the people I didn't know who were about to receive what I had too much of.
>
> In the first house was a man of thirty who had a baby and needed some work clothes. Perfect. I had my clothes to give him and the baby toys and clothes. He needed money for groceries, so I gave him $100.
>
> The next house had three boys all under the age of twelve, so I gave them our TV, VCR, and two video game

consoles. Their mother needed some groceries, so I gave her $100.

The next house had a couple who needed some clothing for the wife and money for a car payment, so I gave her my wife's clothes and $100.

We prayed with each family and told them we came with God. I got such a rush from this that we got home and got more things together to give away. My wife and I are now consistently serving at the homeless center downtown, and I'm going to start teaching art and graphics at the homeless learning center.

Many might question this guy's actions, and some might even criticize him for being too sporadic, but what if this is a simple illustration of the freedom found in obedience? I'm not saying this is how obedience will look in each person's life, but think what would happen if such radical abandonment marked each of our lives.

Listen to this e-mail from Lisa, a woman in our faith family:

For months I've been listening to the Word and banging my head against the wall, trying to reconcile my life with what the gospel demands. I've been trying to find some comfortable alternative between my life now and the radical idea of selling everything I own and leaving the comfortable life to take the gospel to the world. But I've realized there is no comfortable alternative. Risking it all is the only option.

So I'm selling my stuff on the Internet and trying to pay off my debt so that I can give as much as possible. In order to pay off that debt, I really am going to have to sell almost everything I have except the shirt on my back (and maybe a spare!).

I can't wait to see what happens from here. I'm totally unprepared, totally inadequate, totally scared. But I'm ready. Bring it on.

Again, this may seem extreme to some, but the reality is that Lisa's actions correspond far more with Jesus' words in Mark 10 than with the actions of those who sit back and do nothing.

The freedom to give radically has played out in many other ways in our church.

After studying God's care for orphans in James 1:27, we decided to contact the Department of Human Resources and take responsibility for making sure they had enough families to care for the needy children in our county. They needed 150 families, and within two weeks 160 families from our church signed up for foster care and adoption. Today, all across our faith family, men and women are freeing up space in their homes for foster children, while others are spending their savings and investment accounts on adopting children from Birmingham and around the world.

Small groups of all ages across the church have begun sacrificing luxuries for everything from building wells in impoverished communities to buying chickens for starving villages. One Sunday I came back from a city in Indonesia where an earthquake had destroyed thousands of homes. It cost approximately $400 to rebuild a home, so that Sunday, in our response to the Word, I invited people to build homes in Indonesia. People began writing checks and bringing money to the front, and by the end of the day, the church had collected more than $100,000. People who did not have money gave other possessions. One woman gave a wedding ring, saying, "My husband and I do not have much money right now, but I can give this so that a couple in Indonesia can have a home." In the days to come, we worked together with churches in Indonesia to build hundreds of homes while proclaiming the gospel throughout a predominantly Muslim community.

Last month we were studying James 2:14–17 and considering our brothers and sisters around the world who are "without clothes and daily food." In light of the struggling economy, we had been working to conserve money in our budget. As a result we had a surplus of more than $500,000 that we were saving for a rainy day.

Through his Word, God began turning our eyes toward our brothers and sisters in India, a country that is home to 41 percent of the world's poor. Many children there do not live to age five, so we looked for an avenue through which we could serve them. We learned that for about $25,000, we could provide food and water, medical care and education to moms and their babies in a particular village for one year. We found twenty-one churches in impoverished villages all across India, and we started thinking about which ones we might be able to serve. That's when we stepped back and realized, "If there are twenty-one churches in villages that we can connect with, and in each one we can serve starving children and their families for about $25,000, that comes to a total of $525,000. Meanwhile, God has given us more than $500,000."

That led to an exciting decision. We said, "Let's take them all." Two weeks later our church stood and said, "We want to give away all this money for the glory of Christ among our impoverished brothers and sisters."

Please don't misunderstand. The beauty in all these pictures is not just providing for the physical needs of the poor. As we take children into our homes, as our small groups give away their luxuries, and as we go from Birmingham to India and everywhere in between, we are doing it all with the gospel. We are discovering the joy of a radical gospel inside of us that produces radical fruit outside of us. And as we meet needs on earth, we are proclaiming a gospel that transforms lives for eternity. The point is not simply to meet a temporary need or change a startling statistic; the point is to exalt the glory of Christ as we express the gospel of Christ through the radical generosity of our lives.

THE RICH MAN IN ME

As God began uncovering this blind spot in us, my wife and I began looking at the things around us. You see, a couple of years ago, we had lost everything. Our house went underwater in Hurricane Katrina, and all our possessions floated in about ten feet of water for two weeks. After we went back to see what we could salvage, we found ourselves driving away from New Orleans with a few Christmas decorations from the attic to our name.

This was our chance. We could literally start from the bottom and responsibly rebuild our lives more on necessities and less on luxuries. In the days to come, however, we would quickly squander that opportunity.

By the time we moved to Birmingham, where I would begin pastoring, we found ourselves in the throes of buying a house and filling it with stuff. The lure was strong. We didn't buy a mansion, but we did purchase more than we needed. And the more space there is in a house, the more stuff is "necessary" to fill it. It did not take long to find ourselves with twice as much as we once had in New Orleans. In the eyes of the world (even the church world), we had reached the promised land. But I could not get rid of the sinking feeling that we were better able to live out the gospel when we had less.

The lesson I learned is that the war against materialism in our hearts is exactly that: a war. It is a constant battle to resist the temptation to have more luxuries, to acquire more stuff, and to live more comfortably. It requires strong and steady resolve to live out the gospel in the middle of an American dream that identifies success as moving up the ladder, getting the bigger house, purchasing the nicer car, buying the better clothes, eating the finer food, and acquiring more things.

My wife and I have decided we are going to wage the war. We now find ourselves in what seems like a never-ending process of identifying necessities and removing luxuries. We put our house up for sale and began looking for something smaller and simpler. We began the process of adoption again, concluding that our savings were better spent on that which is most important to the heart of God.[35] We are attempting to form a budget that frees up as much as possible to give away.

These things are just the beginning, and we have far to go. So many questions still remain unanswered. What kind of car should I drive? How many clothes do I really need? What luxuries does God intend for my family and me to savor, and what luxuries does God invite us to sacrifice? If we have savings, where is the line between responsible saving (which the Bible certainly advocates) and irresponsible hoarding (which the Bible clearly condemns)?[36] How does all of this affect the way we approach investments, retirement accounts, or life insurance? How much is wise to save for potential future need when brothers and sisters around me (as well as people who haven't even heard the gospel) are threatened by dire present need?

These are not easy questions, and I do not presume to have all the answers. Nor do I claim that there are legalistic measures by which we can or should answer these questions. We must avoid the error of imposing upon ourselves or others laws that are not commanded in Scripture. At the same time, this should not stop us from asking the questions and letting these questions drive us to Christ.

I am discovering in my own life that this is a journey, and along the way I am finding deep joy in depending on Christ for the guidance only he can provide as he produces the fruit of the gospel in my life. More than anything, I don't want to be the rich young man. And I don't want to ignore the fact that the lure toward becoming him is always stronger than I would like to admit.

The Bible says that when Jesus told the rich young man to sell everything he had and give to the poor "the man's face fell. He went away sad, because he had great wealth."[37] Jesus was uncovering a blind spot in his life, and he didn't want to see it. He didn't want to see the extent of his sin, the depth of his bondage to his possessions, or the gravity of the need among the poor. He walked away with full hands but an empty heart. Tragically, he was leaving behind the only one who could bring him the life and joy he so desperately desired.

I don't want to be blind to these things in my own life. And I don't want to leave Christ behind. I don't want to pursue stuff—even stuff in the name of Christianity or stuff in the name of the church—and in the process miss Christ and the pleasures he alone gives in a life free from bondage to the possessions of this world. Ultimately, I don't want to miss eternal treasure because I settle for earthly trinkets. "Where your treasure is," Jesus says, "there your heart will be also."[38] The way we use our money is a barometer of our present spiritual condition. Our neglect of the poor illustrates much about where our hearts lie. But even more than that, the way we use our money is an indicator of our eternal destination. The mark of Christ followers is that their hearts are in heaven and their treasures are spent there.

A Choice

It is easy for the numbers and statistics regarding the poor and needy to seem cold and distant. The idea of billions in poverty or twenty-six thousand children dying from starvation or preventable disease before we lay our heads on our pillows tonight seems hard to imagine.

This was the case for my wife and me when we began the process of adopting our first son. We had read the statistics before…and they were staggering. Millions of orphans in Africa, a number that is rising dramatically as a result of the AIDS crisis that is currently taking the lives of moms and dads across the sub-Saharan plain. Millions of orphans in Asia, many if not most of whom are destined for lives in crime and prostitution if they are not adopted. Millions of orphans in Europe, Latin America, and the United States.

As overwhelming as these numbers were to us, I have to admit they were still just numbers to us before we traveled to Kazakhstan to get our son. It's not that we didn't care. After all, we were going through the adoption process. But the numbers still seemed distant, removed from our daily life in suburban Birmingham.

But everything changed when we made our first trip to the orphanage in Kazakhstan. We saw children playing outside. We walked past their rooms inside. Suddenly those numbers on a page came alive in our hearts. We realized that it was Caleb who was sleeping in one of those cribs, and it was Caleb who was included in those numbers. All at once the numbers became real…and personal.

We learned that orphans are easier to ignore before you know their names. They are easier to ignore before you see their faces. It is easier to pretend they're not real before you hold them in your arms. But once you do, everything changes.

So when you and I hear staggering numbers and statistics

about the poor and needy around us and around the world, we have a choice. We can switch the channels on our mega-TVs and continue our comfortable, untroubled, ordinary, churchgoing lives as if the global poor don't exist. We can let these numbers remain cold, distant, and almost imaginary. Or we can open our eyes and our lives to the realities that surround us and begin considering the faces that are represented by these numbers.

I think about the mass of kids and their parents in the slums of Delhi, India. Families with three, four, five, or more children living in eight-by-twelve-foot shacks. We dodged piles of human feces that littered the ground as we walked on the outskirts of the community. Water was limited, food was scarce, and the urban slum continued for what seemed like miles with no end.

These are the images that come to my mind when I consider what it means to live on less than a dollar or two per day. These are the faces I see when I envision twenty-six thousand children dying today of starvation or preventable diseases.

As I see their faces, I realize that I have a choice. You and I both have a choice.

We can stand with the starving or with the overfed.

We can identify with poor Lazarus on his way to heaven or with the rich man on his way to hell.

We can embrace Jesus while we give away our wealth, or we can walk away from Jesus while we hoard our wealth.

Only time will tell what you and I choose to do with this blind spot of American Christianity in our day.

CHAPTER SEVEN

THERE IS NO
PLAN B

As American Christians, we celebrate the idea that "all men are created equal." This statement from our Declaration of Independence is grounded in the biblical teaching that every person in the world has been formed in the image of God and therefore has intrinsic worth. It's a beautiful idea.

Subtly, however, this equality of persons shifts into an equality of ideas. Just as every person is equally valued, so every idea is equally valid. Applied to faith, this means that in a world where different people have different religious views, all such views should be treated as fundamentally equal.

In this system of thinking, faith is a matter of taste, not of truth. The cardinal sin, therefore, is to claim that one person's belief is true and another person's belief is false. The honorable route is to rest quietly in what you believe and resist the urge to share your beliefs with someone else.

This line of thought has pervaded American Christianity in two particular ways. On one hand, many professing Christians have embraced the universalistic idea that religion is merely a matter of preference or opinion and that in the end all religions are fundamentally the same. People do not have to trust in Christ in order to know God or go to heaven. Therefore, there is no need to encourage someone else to embrace the truth of Christianity.

On the other hand, while some professing Christians have rejected universalism intellectually, practically they may end up leading universalistic lives. They claim Christ is necessary for salvation, yet they live their Christianity in silence, as if people around them in the world will indeed be okay in the end without Christ.

I think that each of us tends toward either intellectual or practical universalism. If you lean toward adopting universalism intellectually, I invite you to hang with me through this chapter. Together, let's explore with open minds the question of what God's Word teaches about this. Similarly, if you lean toward practical universalism, living each day as though it's not absolutely urgent to tell others about Christ, then I invite you to approach this chapter considering the practical and eternal implications of what the Bible teaches.

Let's not forget what's at stake.

We have already seen that more than 4.5 billion people in the world today are without Christ. As if this were not serious enough, more than a billion of these people have never even heard the gospel. So what happens to them when they die? I am convinced that this is one of the most important questions facing Christianity in America today. If people will go to heaven simply based on their native religious preferences, then there is no urgency for any of us to go to them. But if they will not go to heaven because they have never heard of Christ, then there is indescribable urgency for all of us to go to them. If people are dying and going to hell without ever even knowing there is a gospel, then we clearly have no time to waste our lives on an American dream. So what does the Bible say about people who never hear about Jesus?

I invite you to take a brief journey with me through the book of Romans to discover seven truths that help us understand what Scripture teaches about people who have never heard of Jesus.[1] Then I implore you to consider the urgent need before us to forsake the American dream now in favor of radical abandonment to the person and purpose of Christ.

TRUTH 1: ALL PEOPLE HAVE KNOWLEDGE OF GOD

After Paul finished his introduction in Romans, he immediately began exploring how all people have knowledge of God the Father. Starting in Romans 1:18, Paul said that God is revealing himself to all people, "since what may be known about God is plain to them, because God has made it plain to them." He continued, "For since the creation of the world God's invisible qualities—his eternal power and divine nature—have been clearly seen, being understood from what has been made, so that men are without excuse."[2]

In other words, God reveals himself continually and clearly to all people. Paul assumed their knowledge of God when he said, "Although they knew God…"[3] Every person on the face of the earth and every person throughout history—without exception—has knowledge of God the Father. The man in the African jungle, the woman in the Asian village, the nomad in the remotest desert, and the Inuit in the forgotten tundra, regardless of where or how they live, have this in common. All people have knowledge of God because God has revealed himself to them.

Of course, not all people in the world say they believe in God. That leads to the second affirmation.

TRUTH 2: ALL PEOPLE REJECT GOD

Paul said, "Although they knew God, they neither glorified him as God nor gave thanks to him."[4] All people, including you, me, and the man in the African bush, have rejected true knowledge of God. The Bible says we have foolish hearts and futile minds. We have an inherently sinful nature that rebels against the knowledge and the glory of God.[5]

Though this is a fundamental truth of the gospel, it is often overlooked in discussions of what happens to people who never hear about Jesus. We easily forget about the distortions that plague our minds and the idolatry that plagues our hearts because of sin.

I remember discussing this one time with a table full of college students. One of them asked me, "What about a Native American tribe, for example, that originally inhabited parts of America?" She continued, "Maybe that tribe had never heard of Jesus and they didn't have the Bible. But they did have an innate desire to worship, and so they worshiped what they knew—maybe the sun god or something like that." She finished, "They were doing the best they could with the knowledge they had. Isn't that good enough?"

It was a great question, and it drove us back to this fundamental truth that we can't forget, discard, or ignore. All people, including men and women in ancient native tribes, reject true knowledge of God. In the words of Paul, these natives were worshiping created things rather than the Creator.[6]

So does worshiping the sun god count as good enough? The answer is no, according to Paul in Romans 1. People don't get credit before a holy God for worshiping gods they create or imagine. Sun gods, moon goddesses, gods of prosperity—none of them deserves worship. Only God deserves worship. So when we worship these "gods" instead of him, we don't get credit for trying our best. Our idolatry is just not good enough.

This is not a specific indictment of certain native tribes or any other cultures around the world. It is an indictment of all of us. We are all idolaters. Whether in America or Africa or Asia, no one worships God truly, because in our hearts we reject the true God. So there's another truth to consider.

TRUTH 3: ALL PEOPLE ARE GUILTY BEFORE GOD

The first three chapters of the book of Romans contain some of the most depressing verses in all the Bible. Paul built a strong case for the depravity of humankind, using words such as "sinful," "shameful," "evil," "senseless, faithless, heartless," and "ruthless" to describe us.[7]

From Romans 1:18 to 2:16, Paul described the Gentiles who had sinned against God. You can almost see Paul's Jewish readers nodding in agreement at every verse as they think about the wickedness of the heathen around them. But then Paul turned the tables on the Jews in Romans 2:17 and confronted them in their sinfulness. His description of their sin continues all the way into Romans 3, at which point he concluded,

> There is no one righteous, not even one;
>> there is no one who understands,
>> no one who seeks God.
> All have turned away,
>> they have together become worthless;
> there is no one who does good,
>> not even one.[8]

The case has been made, and it is decisive. All people, regardless of religious, cultural, or ethnic background, stand guilty before God. In Paul's words, "Every mouth [is] silenced and the whole world held accountable to God."[9]

Suppose you were to ask me, "What happens to the innocent guy in the middle of Africa who dies without ever hearing the gospel?" My confident answer to you, based on the authority of God's Word, would be, "I believe he will undoubtedly go to heaven. There is no question in my mind."

Now, before some label me a heretic (and others label me a

hero), read back over that last paragraph. Look especially at the hypothetical question: "What happens to the *innocent* guy in the middle of Africa who dies without ever hearing the gospel?" (This is how most people word this question.)

The reality is, the *innocent* guy in Africa will go to heaven because if he is innocent, then he has no need for a Savior to save him from his sin. As a result, he doesn't need the gospel. But there is a significant problem here.

The *innocent* guy doesn't exist…in Africa or anywhere else.

I am always amazed at how we bias this question concerning people who have never heard about Jesus. We give the man in Africa or the woman in Asia or even ourselves in America far too much credit. There are no innocent people in the world just waiting to hear the gospel. Instead there are people all over the world standing guilty before a holy God, and that is the very reason they need the gospel.

All too often we view heaven as the default eternal state for humankind. We assume that our race simply deserves heaven, that God owes heaven to us unless we do something really bad to warrant otherwise. But as we have seen in Romans, this theology is just not true. All people are guilty before God, and as such the default is not heaven but hell. This leads us to our next truth.

TRUTH 4: ALL PEOPLE ARE CONDEMNED FOR REJECTING GOD

Paul concluded his teaching on the sinfulness of human beings by saying, "Therefore no one will be declared righteous in [God's] sight by observing the law; rather, through the law we become conscious of sin."[10] (Hey, I told you that these chapters are depressing!)

Not only is every person guilty before God, but there is also nothing we can do to change this. The more we try to do good, the more we expose our evil. Even our attempts to obey God only further uncover our inability to do so. This applies to you, me, and every other person in the world. As a result, we all stand condemned before God.

This brings us face to face with a fundamental misunderstanding that appears in many answers to the question of what happens to people who never hear about Jesus. Many professing Christians have come to the conclusion that if certain people around the world don't have the opportunity to hear about Jesus, then this automatically excuses them from God's condemnation. Such people will go to heaven because, after all, they never had the opportunity to hear about Jesus.

This line of thinking reflects the intensely emotional nature of this question. We *want* people to be okay when they haven't had the opportunity to hear the gospel. But think with me about the logic of this conclusion. It asserts that people will be with God in heaven for all eternity precisely because they never heard of Christ. Their not hearing about Christ gives them a pass into heaven.

In addition to the lack of biblical evidence for such a pass, consider the practical implications of this idea. If people will go to heaven precisely because they never had the opportunity to hear about Jesus, then the worst thing we could do for their eternal state would be to go to them and tell them about Jesus. That would only increase their chances of going to hell! Before we got there, they were going to heaven; now that we've told them about Jesus, they might go to hell. Thanks a lot!

Imagine encountering an international student newly arrived on a college campus in the United States. You ask her if she has ever heard of Jesus, and with a puzzled look on her face, she responds, "No."

Now, if this girl is headed to heaven precisely because she has never heard about Jesus, then the best thing you could say to her for the sake of her eternity is, "If anyone tries to tell you about Jesus, just put your hands on your ears, start yelling very loudly, and run away."

Obviously this particular methodology is not prescribed in Scripture. But when you follow the logic of the conclusion above, this is the practical result.

Still, though, some will maintain, "Well, is God just in condemning people for not believing in Jesus when they never had the chance to hear about Jesus?" Now that is a really good question, and I believe the answer is no. God would not be just in condemning people for not believing in a Savior they never heard of. But don't forget, people are not ultimately condemned for not believing in Jesus. They are ultimately condemned for rejecting God.

This is the key. There is no question that the billion people who have never heard about Jesus have a different kind of accountability before God than do the rest of us. Those of us who have heard about Jesus have had the opportunity to receive or reject the gospel, and we are responsible for our decision. But regardless of our relative knowledge of the gospel, based on the second truth we've already explored, all people stand condemned fundamentally for rejecting God.[11]

I can imagine tears in Paul's eyes when he comes to Romans 3:20. He has painted a terrifying portrait of humanity's sinfulness. All people know God, all people reject God, all people are guilty before God, and all people stand condemned for rejecting God. But I can also see Paul wiping away those tears as he pens his next words.

TRUTH 5: GOD HAS MADE A WAY OF SALVATION FOR THE LOST

"But now a righteousness from God, apart from law, has been made known.... This righteousness from God comes through faith in Jesus Christ to all who believe."[12] Finally, the good news! Christ died on the cross and rose from the grave, and through him we can be righteous before God and assured of eternal life. God has made a way of salvation for the lost.

Obviously, this truth cannot be taken for granted as being accepted in our world (and even in the church) today. Pluralism dominates the global religious landscape, and the prevailing idea is that if there is a God, he has provided many ways of salvation for the lost.

I remember standing as a student at the front of a classroom on the campus of a state university. It was my day to give a speech, and I spoke on the topic of Christianity. I presented the core truths of the gospel to a class full of fellow college students, most of whom were atheistic or agnostic.

At the conclusion of my speech, the professor opened the floor for questions. Lauren, an honor student and a leader in the student government, was the first to speak. Wise by all the standards that campus had set up, she bluntly asked, "Are you telling me that if I don't believe in the Jesus you're talking about, I will go to hell when I die?"

I'd never heard it put quite that way in front of quite that many people. I began to sweat as a hushed classroom waited for my response. I thought through my words, swallowed hard, and spoke with as much compassion as was in me.

"We all have sin in us that separates us from God. No matter what we do, we can't overcome our own rebellion. That's why Jesus died on the cross—to save us from our sin and ourselves. So, yes, apart from believing in Jesus, you will not go to heaven."

Across the room sighs resounded and eyes rolled as the narrow-minded Christian stood before them. Lauren came up to me after class and said, "That is the most ridiculous thing I've ever heard. Who are you to say that your faith is the only way to God and the rest of us are all going to eternal damnation?" With that, she walked away.

I'd had better days.

That was the first of many conversations with Lauren. In the days to come, she would ask me every question in the book. How do you know God exists? How is Jesus different from other religious leaders? What about people who never hear about Jesus? Each time, I tried the best I could to answer her questions, but often it felt as if my words were bouncing off a brick wall.

After one of these conversations, I was walking across the

campus and began to think, *Do I even really believe this? I don't want to be arrogant or narrow-minded. Am I just believing what I was raised to believe? Is this true? Is Jesus really the only way to God?*

I wrestled with those questions in the months that followed as I never had before. Humbled by this secular university, I left campus at the end of the school year for the summer. Upon returning in the fall, I walked into class on the first day of the semester. There in the front of the room sat Lauren.

She called across the room, "I need to talk to you today."

"Okay," I said. *Oh great,* I thought. *Here we go again.*

Lauren and I talked after class. She told me that during the summer she had come to an understanding of her sinfulness before God. She had also come to an understanding of the sufficiency of Christ to cover her sin. "David," she said, "I have trusted Jesus for my salvation, and now I know that when I die, I'm going to heaven."

God has made a way of salvation for the lost. Not *a* way, but *the* way. And this is the good news—the gospel.

But the question still remains. What about people who never hear what Lauren got to hear? That leads us to our last two truths.

TRUTH 6: PEOPLE CANNOT COME TO GOD APART FROM FAITH IN CHRIST

After writing one of the most mind-boggling and breathtaking paragraphs in all the Bible (Romans 3:21–26), Paul began to explain how God's salvation becomes a reality in our lives.

The Jewish people in his audience were accustomed to following the Law in an effort to know and please God. But in Romans 3:27–31, Paul described how faith in Christ is the only way to be made right before God. He developed this line of thought in depth in Romans 4–5, concluding that "since we have been justified through faith, we have peace with God through our Lord Jesus Christ."[13] Faith in Christ is the only means by which we can be saved.

Some may wonder at this point about how people in the Old Testament were saved. Paul argues in Romans 4–11 that Abraham and others in the Old Testament were saved by grace through faith in the coming Christ. Though they did not know all the details, they were trusting in the redemption God would bring through Christ. Based on their example, some have concluded that people today can also be saved through a general trust in God even though they have never heard of Christ. But Scripture gives no evidence of this once Christ has come. The thrust of the New Testament is that Christ has indeed come and that people must believe in his person and work on the cross for their salvation (Romans 10:9–10).

Now, obviously, if people can't come to God apart from faith in Christ, then this truth is not encouraging for those who have never heard of Christ. Many conclude at this point, "I don't know how, but surely God will make a way for these millions of people to get to heaven even if they haven't heard about Jesus." In the emotional pull of the question, we long for there to be a way for those who have not heard to be saved. We are sure that God in his love would not allow them to go to hell when they haven't even heard of Jesus.

Again, we need to be careful to consider the ramifications of such a conclusion. If we conclude that people can get to heaven apart from faith in Christ, then this would mean there is something else they can do to get to heaven. Such a conclusion would not only undercut the previous truth we saw in Romans; it would also be tantamount to saying to Jesus, "Thank you for what you did on the cross, but we could have gotten to God another way."

Romans (and all of Scripture) is abundantly clear on this point. Faith in Christ is necessary for salvation.[14]

After the first four truths, we finally came to some good news in the fifth truth. But with this sixth truth, we seem to arrive at yet another dismal point. If people cannot come to God apart from faith in Christ, and if more than a billion people have never heard of Christ, then a serious and eternal problem exists. This problem leads us to the final assertion in the book of Romans.

TRUTH 7: CHRIST COMMANDS THE CHURCH TO MAKE THE GOSPEL KNOWN TO ALL PEOPLES

Fast-forward to Romans 10. Paul quoted a verse from the Old Testament book of Joel and then considered some implications.

> "Everyone who calls on the name of the Lord will be saved."
> How, then, can they call on the one they have not believed in? And how can they believe in the one of whom they have not heard? And how can they hear without someone preaching to them? And how can they preach unless they are sent?[15]

These verses don't just depict Paul's rhetorical skill; they are a clear picture of God's redemptive plan. In these three short verses, we see God's design for taking the gospel to all the peoples of the world, including the billion who have never heard the name of Jesus.

In order for us to see it, let's take the verbs from this passage in reverse order. Starting with the last verse, you see that God's plan involves sending his servants. So that's step one in the plan of God—God sends servants.

Then, continuing to move backward in the passage, we see what those servants do. They preach. The servants are sent to preach the gospel. As we have already seen when we considered disciple making, every servant of God is intended to go and proclaim the gospel. This is God's plan. He sends servants, and his servants preach.

Moving one step further back, when his servants preach, people hear. Unless we are preaching to a wall, people will hear us when we preach. So the plan is progressing: God sends servants, his servants preach, and people hear.

When they hear, the previous sentence says, they will believe. Now, this passage is not teaching that every single person who hears the gospel will believe it. That is obviously not true, either scripturally or practically. But this passage is teaching that when we preach and people hear, some of them will believe. We have seen that one day every nation, people, tribe, and language will be represented around the throne of Christ. This means that every people group is going to hear the gospel preached, and someone from every people group is going to trust in Christ for salvation. This gives us great confidence. You can go to the most remote and hostile unreached people group on this planet and preach the gospel to them, and *somebody* is going to believe. God sends servants, his servants preach, people hear, and hearers believe.

The last two steps in God's plan are obvious. When hearers believe, they call on the name of the Lord, and when they call on his name, they will be saved. So there you have it—the simple divine plan for taking the gospel to all peoples of the world.

God sends his servants. → His servants preach. →
People hear. → Hearers believe. →
Believers call. → Everyone who calls is saved.

Now look back at this progression and ask one question: Is there any place where this plan can break down? Think about it. Obviously everyone who calls on the name of the Lord will be saved. No breakdown there. Everyone who believes will call. Many who hear (not all, but many) will believe. People will hear the gospel when we preach it to them. And God is most definitely still in the business of sending his servants.

That means there is only one potential breakdown in this progression—when servants of God do not preach the gospel to all peoples.

We are the plan of God, and there is no plan B.

Of course, God has the power to write the gospel in letters across the clouds so that all people can learn about Jesus and believe in him. But in his infinite wisdom, he has not chosen this route. Instead he has chosen to use us as ambassadors who carry the gospel to people who have never heard the name of Jesus.

Many stories are told today of God revealing Christ in dreams and visions around the world to people who have never heard of Jesus. Consequently, many Christians have begun leaning on the hope that God is using other ways to make the gospel known to people who have never heard of Jesus. But we need to remember something. There is not one verse in the book of Acts where the gospel advances to the lost apart from a human agent. One might point to the vision Cornelius had. But God called Peter to get up and go to Cornelius to help him understand his vision and embrace the gospel.[16] God clearly has decided to use the church—and only the church—as the means by which his gospel will go to the ends of the earth.

No Time to Waste

This, then, is the answer to our question of what happens to people who never hear about Jesus. All people know God, and all people reject God. All people are guilty before God, and all people are condemned for rejecting God. God has made a way of salvation for the lost, and people cannot come to God apart from faith in Christ. As a result, Christ commands the church to make the gospel known to all peoples.

If this is true, then the implications for our lives are huge. If more than a billion people today are headed to a Christless eternity and have not even heard the gospel, then we don't have time to waste our lives on an American dream. Not if we have all been commanded to take this gospel to them. The tendency in our culture is to sit around debating this question, but in the end our goal is not to try to find an answer to it; our goal is to alleviate the question altogether.

More than five thousand people groups, totaling approximately 1.5 billion people, are currently classified as "unreached" and "unengaged." "Unreached" means that a people group does not contain an indigenous community of evangelical Christians with adequate numbers and resources to spread the gospel within the people group. "Unengaged" means no church or organization is actively working within that people group to spread the gospel. In other words, for these 1.5 billion unreached and unengaged peoples, almost every individual within them is born, lives, and dies without ever hearing the gospel. Even worse, no one is currently doing anything to change their situation. No one.

One of my good friends spent time recently among unreached and unengaged peoples in Southeast Asia. As he talked with villagers in one remote area, he tried to uncover their core beliefs. He asked them, "How were we created?"

They responded, "We don't know."

He asked, "Who sends the rain for the crops?"

They responded, "We don't know that either."

Then he asked, "What happens when we die?"

They looked back at him and said, "No one has come to tell us about that yet."

Soon thereafter he found himself in another remote village with people who had never heard the gospel. They were warm and hospitable, and they invited him to share a drink with them. One man went into his small shop and reappeared moments later with a classic red Coke can. Immediately, it hit home with my friend. A soft-drink company in Atlanta has done a better job getting brown sugar water to these people than the church of Jesus Christ has done in getting the gospel to them.

Consider just one of these unreached people groups. The Bedouins of Algeria are 1.4 million strong. They live in portable tents covered with goat hair. They have little food and often live in unhealthy conditions. They are 100 percent Muslim. No Christians. No churches. No missionaries. No gospel. No Jesus. Meanwhile, God has saved you and me by his grace. He has not only given us knowledge about Christ, but he has also given us the presence of Christ and the promise of Christ to provide us with everything we need to take the gospel to them. Now imagine what it would be like to look into a pair of Bedouin eyes and for the first time introduce this person to Christ.

This is a cause worth living for. It is a cause worth dying for. It is a cause worthy of moving urgently on. We have the gospel of Christ in us, and we do not have time to waste. Some wonder if it is unfair for God to allow so many to have no knowledge of the gospel. But there is no injustice in God. The injustice lies in Christians who possess the gospel and refuse to give their lives to making it known among those who haven't heard. That is unfair.

I find it interesting that one of the most common questions asked today among Christians is "What is God's will for my life?" or "How do I find God's will for my life?" Many Christians have almost assumed the attitude that they would obey God if he would just show them what he wanted them to do.

In the middle of a Christian culture asking, "How do I find God's will for my life?" I bring good news. His will is not lost.

With 1.4 million Bedouins in Algeria who have never even heard the gospel, it makes little sense for us to sit over here asking, "What do you want me to do, God?" The answer is clear. The will of God is for you and me to give our lives urgently and recklessly to making the gospel and the glory of God known among all peoples, particularly those who have never even heard of Jesus.

The question, therefore, is not "Can we find God's will?" The question is "Will we obey God's will?"

Will we refuse to sit back and wait for some tingly feeling to go down our spines before we rise up and do what we have already been commanded to do?

Will we risk everything—our comfort, our possessions, our safety, our security, our very lives—to make the gospel known among unreached peoples?

Such rising up and such risk taking are the unavoidable, urgent results of a life that is radically abandoned to Jesus.

CHAPTER EIGHT

LIVING WHEN
DYING IS GAIN

THE RISK AND REWARD OF THE RADICAL LIFE

Amid the many facets of the American dream that contradict the core of the gospel, one ideal Americans have embraced coincides subtly with the words of Christ. As James Adams was coining the phrase "American dream," Franklin Roosevelt was emphasizing how Americans will postpone immediate gratification and even endure hard sacrifices if they are convinced their future will be better than their past. Americans are willing to take great risks, he said, if they believe it will accomplish great reward.

In similar words Jesus said to his followers, "Whoever finds his life will lose it, and whoever loses his life for my sake will find it."[1] Jesus clearly acknowledged that following him involves risking the safety, security, and satisfaction we have found in this world. But in the end, Jesus said, following him leads to a radical reward that this world can never offer. This begs a question from each of us:

do we believe the reward found in Jesus is worth the risk of following him?

GO TO NEED

Jesus' challenge to lose our lives came at the end of a startling speech he made to his disciples, as told in Matthew 10. Sending the disciples into the world, Jesus outlined the risks they would have to undertake in following him.

He told his disciples that they would be surrounded by great need. His instructions? "Heal the sick, raise the dead, cleanse those who have leprosy, drive out demons."[2] Just imagine the people that the disciples were going to encounter. The diseased, the dying, the despised, and the dangerous. Not exactly the most appealing group to be around.

Some members of our faith family recently went to southern Africa to provide a medical clinic in various impoverished communities. Upon their arrival in the country, one of their vehicles was hijacked. The driver was pistol-whipped and thrown into the trunk of another car as the assailants drove off with most of our team's luggage. By God's grace, no one else was hurt, and the driver recovered.

The team knew the trip involved risk, though they certainly hadn't planned on getting hijacked. Instead, the risk they had considered involved the medical clinics they would be providing. The team knew they would be working with countless patients infected with HIV, the virus that leads to AIDS. They had discussed all the precautions they would need to take, but they knew there was no guarantee they could avoid accidentally being stuck with a needle.

After getting settled in, they began providing the clinics. These were packed every day as men and women with health needs traveled for miles to receive medical attention. As expected, many of the patients were infected with HIV, and just a few days into the trip, it happened.

One of the members of our faith family was serving a woman infected with HIV, and our team member was accidentally stuck with the needle she had been using. As if this were not enough, the same thing happened to a second team member hours later.

Both knew the gravity of what had occurred. It was possible that either one or both of them could have HIV at that point. It was possible that they had just seen their lives change in a very serious way. And that makes their response all the more astounding. "We're glad it happened to us and no one else," they both said. "And if these clinics were used by God to lead someone to Christ, then it was all worth it."

Our partner on the ground in Africa e-mailed us after the group returned home. He reported, "After you guys left, the community was abuzz about the clinic and how much it meant to them that the Lord saw their needs and sent you guys. After you left, the community began thanking the Lord, and many people came to Christ. Isn't God good?"

Yes, he is good. He is good even when he calls you and me to places that are dirty and disease ridden. He is good even when we end up possibly sharing in the diseases of the people we go to serve. He is good because he has met us at our deepest need and now uses us to show his glory and to advance his gospel among the places of greatest need in the world.

GO TO DANGER

I can imagine the looks on the disciples' faces when the next words came out of Jesus' mouth: "I am sending you out like sheep among wolves."[3] Sheep are among the most helpless of all domesticated animals. They are also some of the most senseless. Harmless noises can send them into a frenzy, and when they face danger, they have no defense mechanism. All they can do is run, and unfortunately they are slow. As a result, the dumbest thing a sheep can do is to wander into a pack of wolves. So why in the world was Jesus, the good shepherd (John 10:11), the great Shepherd (Hebrews 13:20), telling his sheep to hang out with wolves?

Jesus was saying to his disciples then—and, by implication, to you and me now—"I am sending you to dangerous places, where you will find yourself in the middle of evil, vicious people. And you will be there by my design." Jesus told them, "Go to great danger, and let it be said of you what people would say of sheep wandering into the middle of wolves. 'They're crazy! They're clueless! They have no idea what kind of danger they are getting into!' This is what it means to be my disciple."

We don't think like this. We say things such as, "The safest place to be is in the center of God's will." We think, *If it's dangerous, God must not be in it. If it's risky, if it's unsafe, if it's costly, it must not be God's will.* But what if these factors are actually the criteria by which we determine something *is* God's will? What if we began to look at the design of God as the most dangerous option before us? What if the center of God's will is in reality the most unsafe place for us to be?

I met a Christian brother from the Batak tribe of northern Sumatra in Indonesia. He told me the story of how his tribe had come to know Christ. Years ago a missionary couple had come to his village to share the gospel. The tribe was 100 percent Muslim. Talk about sheep in the middle of wolves. The tribal leaders captured this missionary couple, then murdered and cannibalized them.

Years later another missionary came to their tribe and again began sharing the gospel. The tribal leaders recognized that the story he told was exactly what the former couple had shared. This time they decided to listen. After they listened, they believed. Within a short time, the entire tribe was converted to Christ. This believer told me that today there are more than three million Christians among the Batak tribe of northern Sumatra.

When I first heard this story, the immediate questions that came to my mind were *Would I be willing for my wife and me to be that first missionary couple? Would I be willing to be killed and cannibalized so that those who come after me would see people come to Christ?*

These are the kinds of questions Matthew 10 poses for each of us. Are we willing, as the first disciples were, to be the first to go into danger and possibly even to die there in order that those who come behind us might experience the fruit of our sacrifice? What if such sacrifice is exactly what it will take for many of the unreached people in the world who are presently hostile to the gospel to one day surrender their hearts to Jesus?

BETRAYED, HATED, AND PERSECUTED

Jesus continued by telling his disciples they would be betrayed. "Brother will betray brother to death, and a father his child; children will rebel against their parents and have them put to death."[4] This was not an encouraging send-off for the disciples. Family members might turn on them, and friends might end up becoming their greatest enemies.

I will not soon forget Sahil's testimony. He and his wife both grew up in Muslim homes in India. She came to Christ and then introduced Sahil to Christ. But as soon as their families discovered they had become Christians, they were forced to flee their community at the risk of their lives.

In the years that followed, they grew in Christ and in their desire to see their family know Christ. Slowly they began to initiate renewed contact with the family members they loved. And slowly their family members began to respond. They eventually welcomed Sahil and his wife back to their community, and from all appearances things were going well.

Then one day Sahil dropped off his wife for a meal with her family while he went to be with his family. His wife sat down at the table with her family and began to drink and eat. Within moments she was dead. Her own parents had poisoned her.

You will be betrayed.

You will be betrayed, and you will be hated. "All men will hate you because of me."[5] Now, "all men" obviously doesn't mean that every person on earth will hate you. But the picture is clear. Whether it is your family, the government, the religious establishment, or someone else, you will be hated.

Again, we don't think like this. "If we would all just become like Jesus, the world would love us," we say. The reality is that if we really become like Jesus, the world will hate us. Why? Because the world hated him.

Jesus said next, "When you are persecuted in one place, flee to another."[6] Not *if* you are persecuted but *when* you are persecuted. Lest we think this is referring only to Jesus' immediate disciples and not to us, Paul told us later, "*Everyone* who wants to live a godly life in Christ Jesus will be persecuted."[7]

The reason we know that we will be betrayed, hated, and persecuted is because Jesus himself was betrayed, hated, and persecuted. The more our lives are conformed to his, the more we will receive what he received in this world. This is why Jesus said, "A student is not above his teacher, nor a servant above his master.... If the head of the house has been called Beelzebub, how much more the members of his household!"[8]

This is the unavoidable conclusion of Matthew 10. To everyone wanting a safe, untroubled, comfortable life free from danger, stay away from Jesus. The danger in our lives will always increase in proportion to the depth of our relationship with Christ.

Maybe this is why we sit back and settle for a casual relationship with Christ and routine religion in the church. It is safe there, and the world likes us there. The world likes us when we are pursuing everything they are pursuing, even if we do put a Christian label on it. As long as Christianity looks like the American dream, we will have few problems in this world.

But if we identify with Christ, we will lose much in this world. Jesus said this himself: "Everyone who is fully trained will be like his teacher."[9] These words should frighten us. They should frighten us because our Teacher was mocked, beaten, scourged, spit upon, and nailed to a cross. Do we really want to be like him?

See what Paul said to the church: "It has been granted to you on behalf of Christ not only to believe on him, but also to suffer for him."[10] This is astonishing. Paul essentially said, "Christ has given you a gift of suffering. Come to Christ and get a great gift—suffering." This is not your typical evangelistic invitation. Bow your heads, close your eyes, pray to receive Christ, and you will receive suffering. It almost seems as though Paul was joking.

But it's not a joke.

It's Christianity.

It's Christian history. Persecution and suffering as we see today in the Middle East, Asia, and Africa have marked followers of Christ from the beginning of the church. In the nearly three hundred years before Christianity was legalized by Constantine, followers of Christ faced terrible persecution. For ten generations, Christians dug nearly six hundred miles of catacombs beneath and around the city of Rome. Catacombs were underground tombs where Christians often gathered in secret for worship. Thousands and thousands of Christians were buried there as a result of intense persecution.

Archaeologists who have explored the catacombs have found a common inscription scattered throughout them. The inscription was the Greek word *ichthus,* which was used as an acrostic for "Jesus Christ, God's Son, the Savior." You might recognize this sign because now these fish symbols are scattered across the backs of cars belonging to Christians. How far we have come when we paste this symbol identified with martyred brothers and sisters in the first century onto the backs of our SUVs and luxury sedans in the twenty-first century.

TROOP CARRIER OR LUXURY LINER?

The language of Matthew 10 envisions Jesus as a military commander sending soldiers out on a mission. He summoned his disciples, and then he sent them out. In light of the needs before them and the danger around them, the disciples knew they were entering into battle.

In the late 1940s, the United States government commissioned William Francis Gibbs to work with United States Lines to construct an eighty-million-dollar troop carrier for the navy. The purpose was to design a ship that could speedily carry fifteen thousand troops during times of war. By 1952, construction on the SS *United States* was complete. The ship could travel at forty-four knots (about fifty-one miles per hour), and she could steam ten thousand miles without stopping for fuel or supplies. She could outrun any other ship and travel nonstop anywhere in the world in less than ten days. The SS *United States* was the fastest and most reliable troop carrier in the world.

The only catch is, she never carried troops. At least not in any official capacity. The ship was put on standby once during the

Cuban missile crisis in 1962, but otherwise she was never used in all her capacity by the U.S. Navy.

Instead the SS *United States* became a luxury liner for presidents, heads of state, and a variety of other celebrities who traveled on her during her seventeen years of service. As a luxury liner, she couldn't carry fifteen thousand people. Instead she could house just under two thousand passengers. Those passengers could enjoy the luxuries of 695 staterooms, 4 dining salons, 3 bars, 2 theaters, 5 acres of open deck with a heated pool, 19 elevators, and the comfort of the world's first fully air-conditioned passenger ship. Instead of a vessel used for battle during wartime, the SS *United States* became a means of indulgence for wealthy patrons who desired to coast peacefully across the Atlantic.

Things look radically different on a luxury liner than they do on a troop carrier. The faces of soldiers preparing for battle and those of patrons enjoying their bonbons are radically different. The conservation of resources on a troop carrier contrasts sharply with the opulence that characterizes the luxury liner. And the pace at which the troop carrier moves is by necessity much faster than that of the luxury liner. After all, the troop carrier has an urgent task to accomplish; the luxury liner, on the other hand, is free to casually enjoy the trip.

When I think about the history of the SS *United States,* I wonder if she has something to teach us about the history of the church. The church, like the SS *United States,* has been designed for battle. The purpose of the church is to mobilize a people to accomplish a mission. Yet we seem to have turned the church as troop carrier into the church as luxury liner. We seem to have organized ourselves, not to engage in battle for the souls of peoples around the world, but to indulge ourselves in the peaceful comforts of the world. This makes me wonder what would happen if we looked squarely in the face of a world with 4.5 billion people going to hell and twenty-six thousand children dying every day of starvation and preventable diseases, and we decided it was time to move this ship into battle instead of sitting back on the pool deck while we wait for the staff to serve us more hors d'oeuvre.

Are we willing to obey the orders of Christ? Are we willing to be like him? Are we willing to risk our lives to go to great need and to great danger—whether it's in the inner cities around us, the difficult neighbor across the street, the disease-ridden communities in Africa, or the hostile regions in the Middle East? Are we willing to fundamentally alter our understanding of Christianity from a luxury-liner approach that seeks more comforts in the world to a troop-carrier approach that forsakes comforts in the world to accomplish an eternally significant task and achieve an eternally satisfying reward?

A GREATER REWARD

This is where Christ dramatically deviates from the American dream. Yes, Jesus promises great reward, but his reward looks much different than what we might expect. The reward of the American dream is safety, security, and success found in more comfort, better stuff, and greater prosperity. But the reward of Christ trumps all these things and beckons us to live for an eternal safety, security, and satisfaction that far outweigh everything this world has to offer us.

Jesus followed his humbling call for his disciples to go to great need and great danger with overwhelming promises of his love and care for them. Three times he told them, "Do not be afraid."[11]

How is it possible for sheep going into the middle of wolves not to be afraid? How can Jesus say that his disciples would be betrayed, hated, and persecuted but they would not need to fear?

HIS SOVEREIGNTY, OUR SAFETY

Jesus reminded his disciples that their safety was not found in the comforts of this world but in the control of a sovereign God over this world. Jesus asked his disciples, "Are not two sparrows sold for a penny? Yet not one of them will fall to the ground apart from the will of your Father."[12] We can rest confident in the fact that nothing will happen to us in this world apart from the gracious will of a sovereign God. Nothing.

This is what I love about Stephen in the book of Acts. According to Scripture, he was the first Christian martyr. As we learn in Acts 7, he was stoned by the Sanhedrin religious council—a remarkable picture of what it means to share in the sufferings of Christ.[13] But what is even more remarkable in this story is what happened as a result of Stephen's death. Luke wrote, "On that day a great persecution broke out against the church at Jerusalem, and all except the apostles were scattered throughout Judea and Samaria." Then Luke wrote three verses later, "Those who had been scattered preached the word wherever they went."[14] In other words, as a result of Stephen's suffering and death, the church multiplied throughout Judea and Samaria.

Do you see what was happening here? Satan's strategy to stop God's people through the stoning of Stephen only served to accomplish God's purpose through the scattering of the church.

This is the testimony of all Scripture. From the story of Job to Paul's description of Satan's attack in his life in 2 Corinthians 12, we see how Satan not only acts within the sovereign permission of God but also ends up accomplishing the sovereign purposes of God. Indeed, this is what the Cross is all about. Satan's strategy to defeat the Son of God only served to provide salvation for sinners.

We have nothing to fear, because God is sovereign.

His Love, Our Security

The reward of Christ also involves a greater security than this world can ever provide. After Jesus talked about the sparrows in Matthew 10, he reminded his disciples of his love for them. In his words, "Even the very hairs of your head are all numbered. So don't be afraid; you are worth more than many sparrows."[15] Jesus knows every detail of our lives, and he cares for us deeply. This is the second reason that we have nothing to fear.

A few weeks ago we sent out a family from our church to an impoverished country overseas. Several months earlier Craig and Amy had shared with me their desire to sell their home in Birmingham and take their three kids to another part of the world where they could better glorify God. As we talked, I encouraged them to persevere through what I anticipated would be difficult times ahead. A couple of months after that initial meeting, we met again, and Craig shared with me the setbacks they had experienced. Since we had last talked, one of their grandmothers had died, one of their brothers had been rushed to the hospital with a stroke, they had been robbed, and they had been in a car wreck.

On top of all this, they had been dealing with various health problems that Amy was experiencing. This was threatening to limit their ability to go overseas because Amy's health might require her to live in a particular climate that would be more conducive to her health. With tears in their eyes, Craig and Amy shared how God had led their hearts to one particular country. When they went to her doctor to ask his opinion on how Amy would fare in that climate, the doctor said that she would actually do even better in that climate than in the United States.

Indeed, God knows every detail of our lives, and when we step out in faith to follow him, he will show us that our greatest security is not found in the comforts we can manufacture in this world but in the faithful provision of the only one who knows our needs and the only one who is able to meet our needs in every way.

His Presence, Our Satisfaction

Out of all the amazing statements of Jesus in Matthew 10, this one may be the most astounding and most important: "Do not be afraid of those who kill the body but cannot kill the soul. Rather, be afraid of the One who can destroy both soul and body in hell."[16]

Frankly, this seems a weird way to encourage disciples who

were risking their lives in obedience to him. Jesus was telling them—and us—that we need to fear God, not people. God is the ultimate Judge, and he holds our eternity in his hands. People don't have that power, so we need not fear them.

Let me paraphrase what Jesus was saying here to help us feel the weight of it. Jesus was telling disciples who would face certain persecution and suffering, "Don't be afraid of people. The worst they can do is kill you."

What kind of encouragement is that?

We say, "Well, if I go to this place, I could be killed."

Jesus replies, "That's all?"

We don't need to be afraid to go anywhere in this world, because the worst that could happen is that we might be killed. And this is supposed to comfort us!

The only way this can comfort us is if we have already died with Christ. The only way this can encourage us is if we are so focused on an eternal God that temporal human beings strike no fear in us. In the words of Paul, "To live is Christ and to die is gain."[17] Clearly, the only way death can be a reward is if dying really is gain.

THEY DID NOT LOVE THEIR LIVES

Church history is replete with stories of men and women who, in the words of Revelation, "did not love their lives so much as to shrink from death."[18]

John Paton (1824–1907) is relatively unknown among Christians today. He served for ten years as the pastor of a growing

Scottish church, but God began to burden his heart for the New Hebrides, a group of Pacific islands filled with cannibalistic peoples and no knowledge of the gospel.

He set his heart on one island in particular. Twenty years earlier two missionaries had gone to that island. They were killed and cannibalized. So it was no surprise that many dissuaded Paton from even the thought of following in these missionaries' footsteps. Paton wrote, "Amongst many who sought to deter me, was one dear old Christian gentleman, whose crowning argument always was, 'The Cannibals! you will be eaten by Cannibals!'"

John Paton replied to this man, "Mr. Dickson, you are advanced in years now, and your own prospect is soon to be laid in the grave, there to be eaten by worms; I confess to you, that if I can but live and die serving and honouring the Lord Jesus, it will make no difference to me whether I am eaten by Cannibals or by worms; and in the Great Day my resurrection body will arise as fair as yours in the likeness of our risen Redeemer."

The old man left the room, exclaiming, "After that I have nothing more to say!"[19]

At the age of thirty-three, John Paton traveled to the New Hebrides with his wife. The journey was not easy. His wife and newborn child died within months after arriving, and he found himself alone, digging their graves with his bare hands. He faced threat after threat upon his life. But in the years to come, countless cannibals across the New Hebrides came to know the peace of Christ, and the church across Australia, Scotland, and the Western world was challenged to rise up and make the gospel known among the peoples who are toughest to reach.

Jim Elliot (1927–56) has a similar story, though his life ended much differently. Elliot was convinced that God was leading him to the Huaorani Indians, a tribe known for killing any outsiders who tried to approach them. They had never heard the gospel, and Elliot found himself joined with a few other men who believed it was their responsibility to take the gospel to them. Elliot was a gifted preacher, and many in the church tried to dissuade him from going. It was too risky, they said.

Elliot wrote in his journal, "Surely those who know the great passionate heart of Jehovah must deny their own loves to share in the expression of His." He continued,

> Consider the call from the Throne above, "Go ye," and
> from round about, "Come over and help us," and even
> the call from the damned souls below, "Send Lazarus to
> my brothers, that they come not to this place." Impelled,
> then, by these voices, I dare not stay home while Quichuas
> perish. So what if the well-fed church in the homeland
> needs stirring? They have the Scriptures, Moses, and the
> Prophets, and a whole lot more. Their condemnation is
> written on their bank books and in the dust on their
> Bible covers. American believers have sold their lives to
> the service of Mammon, and God has His rightful way
> of dealing with those who succumb to the spirit of
> Laodicea.[20]

On January 8, 1956, Elliot and his four comrades met with members of the Huaorani at a designated beachhead. They were greeted with spears, and each of the men died that day at the hands of tribesmen. Should Elliot have listened to those who told him not to take the risk? You be the judge. In the days to come, Elliot's wife, Elisabeth, would be a part of leading to Christ the very men who speared her husband, and since that day the peace of Christ has come to reign in this tribe.

Consider one other example. Few Christians know of C. T. Studd (1860–1931), a wealthy Englishman who sold everything he had to take the gospel to the nations. Studd's family and various Christian workers were brought in to dissuade him from going overseas. But he went anyway, first to China and then to India. At the age of fifty, he decided retirement was not an option for the Christian, so he went to Sudan, where he spent the remaining years of his life. His grave would become the steppingstone for the Worldwide Evangelization Crusade, which spread gospel seeds all across Africa, Asia, and South America.

Listen to the reward Studd was living for, as expressed in some of the last words he wrote before he died:

> Too long have we been waiting for one another to begin! The time for waiting is past!… Should such men as we fear? Before the whole world, aye, before the sleepy, lukewarm, faithless, namby-pamby Christian world, we will dare to trust our God,…and we will do it with His joy unspeakable singing aloud in our hearts. We will a thousand times sooner die trusting only in our God than live trusting in man. And when we come to this position the battle is already won, and the end of the glorious

campaign in sight. We will have the real Holiness of God, not the sickly stuff of talk and dainty words and pretty thoughts; we will have a Masculine Holiness, one of daring faith and works for Jesus Christ.[21]

LIFE IS RADICAL WHEN DEATH IS REWARD

John Paton, Jim Elliot, and C. T. Studd all illustrate one fundamental truth: your life is free to be radical when you see death as reward. This is the essence of what Jesus taught in Matthew 10, and I believe it is *the key* to taking back your faith from the American dream.

The key is realizing—and believing—that this world is not your home. If you and I ever hope to free our lives from worldly desires, worldly thinking, worldly pleasures, worldly dreams, worldly ideals, worldly values, worldly ambitions, and worldly acclaim, then we must focus our lives on another world. Though you and I live in the United States of America now, we must fix our attention on "a better country—a heavenly one."[22] Though you and I find ourselves surrounded by the lure of temporary pleasure, we must fasten our affections on the one who promises eternal treasure that will never spoil or fade. If your life or my life is going to count on earth, we must start by concentrating on heaven. For then, and only then, will you and I be free to take radical risk, knowing that what awaits us is radical reward.

Genessa Wells was a young woman fresh out of college with all the potential in the world. With many opportunities before her, she decided to go to the Middle East among people who had never heard the gospel. Before she went, Genessa wrote to her friends, "I could give up [on going overseas] and get married and become a music teacher. All of this is very noble and to be quite honest, sounds good to me! But in my heart, I want to change my world—more than I want a husband and more than I want comfort. I need…to tell others about Jesus."

Genessa wound up working among the Egyptians, with Palestinians in refugee camps in Jordan, with Muslims in France, and with Bedouins in the desert.

Following all this, she wrote, "I honestly would not want to be anywhere else but here, where God has put me. He gives me more than I can imagine." Six months later, in her last e-mail home, she wrote, "It seems that everything we do comes down to one thing: His glory. I pray that all our lives reflect that."

Two weeks after she wrote these words, Genessa Wells died in a bus accident in the predawn darkness of Egypt's Sinai desert.[23]

Most people in our culture look upon this story as a tragedy. A young woman spending the last days of her life in the remote Egyptian desert, only to die in a bus accident. Think of all the potential she had. Think of all she could have accomplished. Think of all she could have done if she had not gone there.

The perspective of Christ is much different. According to Matthew 10, the story of Genessa Wells is not a story of tragedy but a story of reward.

Reward? How can a young woman's dying in the desert on the other side of the world be a reward?

Here's how. In the instant after Genessa Wells breathed her last breath in Egypt's Sinai Desert, she was ushered into the presence of Christ. There she glimpsed his glory in an amazing beauty that you and I cannot even begin to fathom. And do you know where Genessa Wells is today? She is in the same place. Do you know where Genessa Wells will be ten billion years from now? In the same place, beholding the great glory of her God and experiencing a reward that comes to those who believe that to live is Christ and to die is gain. Rest assured, Genessa does not regret missing one moment of the American dream in light of the reward she now experiences.

This, we remember, is the great reward of the gospel: God himself. When we risk our lives to run after Christ, we discover the safety that is found only in his sovereignty, the security that is found only in his love, and the satisfaction that is found only in his presence. This is the eternally great reward, and we would be foolish to settle for anything less.

When we consider the promises of Christ, risking everything we are and everything we have for his sake is no longer a matter of sacrifice. It's just common sense. Following Christ is not sacrificial as much as it is smart. Jim Elliot once said, "He is no fool who gives what he cannot keep to gain what he cannot lose."

Radical obedience to Christ is not easy; it is dangerous. It is not smooth sailing aboard a luxury liner; it is sacrificial duty aboard a troop carrier. It's not comfort, not health, not wealth, and not prosperity in this world. Radical obedience to Christ risks losing all these things. But in the end, such risk finds its reward in Christ. And he is more than enough for us.

CHAPTER NINE

THE RADICAL
EXPERIMENT

ONE YEAR TO A LIFE TURNED UPSIDE DOWN

Ex•per•i•ment *n.*: a course of action taken under controlled conditions in order to test a claim.

Throughout this book we have explored a variety of bold claims about our purpose in life that are contained in the gospel yet contradicted by the American dream. Claims such as these: Real success is found in radical sacrifice. Ultimate satisfaction is found not in making much of ourselves but in making much of God. The purpose of our lives transcends the country and culture in which we live. Meaning is found in community, not individualism; joy is found in generosity, not materialism; and truth is found in Christ, not universalism. Ultimately, Jesus is a reward worth risking everything to know, experience, and enjoy.

But claims such as these remain theories until they are tested. That is the reason for the experiment. As you test a claim, you discover either its futility or its reality. And once you discover a claim's reality, then you're more likely to adjust your perspective, rearrange your thoughts, and alter your life around that truth. It will turn your life upside down—or, really, right side up.

So I challenge you to an experiment. I dare you to test the claims contained in the gospel, maybe in a way you have never done before. I invite you to see if radical obedience to the commands of Christ is more meaningful, more fulfilling, and more gratifying than the American dream. And I guarantee that if you complete this experiment, you will possess an insatiable desire to spend the rest of your life in radical abandonment to Christ for his glory in all the world.

We'll call it the Radical Experiment.

ONE YEAR

The experiment is for one year. Now, I realize that such a time line does not coincide with conventional wisdom. Contemporary church-growth philosophers tell me in magazines, articles, fliers, and gimmicks that to be effective, we must organize everything we do in no more than six- or eight-week segments. Churchgoers today want short-term commitments with long-term benefits.

I am thankful Christian history has not always operated on this philosophy. David Brainerd (1718–47) spent years suffering through loneliness, depression, and pain before he saw God bring revival among Native Americans in the Northeast. William Carey (1761–1834) stayed committed to preaching the gospel for seven years before he saw one person saved in India. John Hyde

(1865–1912) wore his body down through long nights of prayer and fasting in order to see people come to Christ in one of the hardest mission fields in the world, the Punjab. The examples of Brainerd, Carey, and Hyde should inspire us to ask, "What if long-term benefits are actually reserved for long-term commitments?"

Even the world believes this. Why else would graduating high school seniors commit, at a minimum, four years and thousands of dollars to further their education? Why else would law and medical students suffer through tireless work and grueling schedules? Why else would musicians practice their instruments day after day, or why else would athletes train year after year for a sport? People make long-term commitments all the time out of a desire for long-term benefit. I bet you have made more than one long-term commitment that you look back on with satisfaction.

So my challenge to you is to use one year of your life to radically alter the remainder of your life. I believe it is important, though, to keep the focus on one year, because there are some things you can do for a year that you may not be able to sustain for multiple years. And there are some things you can postpone for one year that you may not be able to postpone for longer. So the challenge here is not forever.

The challenge is for one year, and it involves five components. I dare you over the next year to…

1. pray for the entire world;
2. read through the entire Word;
3. sacrifice your money for a specific purpose;
4. spend your time in another context;
5. commit your life to a multiplying community.

I believe—no, I *know*—that if you stick to these challenges for a whole year, you will find yourself coming alive like never before. You will know the incomparable thrill of being a part of what God is up to where you live and around the world. You will be ready to shed forever the unworthy parts of the American dream and hold on to the beautiful and lasting dream that God has designed for you.

Let's get to those five components that will take you there.

PRAY FOR THE ENTIRE WORLD

I realize that at first this may sound general, vague, ambiguous, even a bit out of reach. You may be thinking, *Can I as an individual really pray specifically and effectively for the entire world?* Let me show you what I mean and why it's so important.

In a world where more than 4.5 billion people are without Christ and more than a billion are on the edge of starvation, we have to begin somewhere. So where? Jesus answers that question for us. In Matthew 9 we see him surrounded by the multitudes and moved with compassion because they were "harassed and helpless, like sheep without a shepherd." So he turned to his disciples and said, "The harvest is plentiful but the workers are few. Ask the Lord of the harvest, therefore, to send out workers into his harvest field."[1]

Do these words surprise you? They do me...for two reasons. First, in light of all the sick, poor, and needy around Jesus, I would have expected him to immediately start giving marching orders to his disciples. "Peter, you go to that person. John, you care for that guy. Andrew, you help her over there." But that's not what he said. Yes, as we see in Matthew 10, he gave them the instructions that we looked at in the last chapter. But before he told them to do anything else, Jesus told them to pray.

What is even more surprising, though, is what Jesus told them to pray for. I would have expected Jesus to say, "You guys see the need. The harvest is plentiful. So pray for these people who are harassed and helpless. Pray for them." But that isn't what he said. Jesus didn't say to pray for those who were lost. Instead he told the disciples to pray for the church.

Why do you think Jesus would look at the crowds around him, with all their deep needs, and then turn to his disciples and tell them to pray for themselves? The answer is humbling. When Jesus looked at the harassed and helpless multitudes, apparently his concern was not that the lost would not come to the Father. Instead his concern was that his followers would not go to the lost.

Now think about it. What happens when you and I take these words from Jesus and put them in a world where more than a billion people have still not heard the gospel? A fundamental reality snaps into focus: we are not praying. This is the only possible explanation for how there can be such great need yet so few workers. The multitudes are waiting to hear, and our most urgent need is to pray for the Lord of the harvest to send out Christians into the harvest field.

This is the step that you and I are most likely to overlook and yet the one that is most dangerous for us to ignore. In the gospel we have seen the depth of our inadequacy and the extent of our inability to accomplish anything of eternal value apart from the power of

God. We are a planning, strategizing, implementing people, yet radical obedience to Christ requires that we be a praying people.

Not long ago a friend of mine spent a couple of weeks in South Korea, a country that has seen explosive Christian growth in recent years. Over the last century, some estimate, almost half the population in that country has come to Christ. Church leaders there have been intentional about pointing to the power of God in prayer as the reason they have seen such widespread spiritual awakening.

My friend was staying in a hotel, and one morning around four o'clock, he was awakened by a loud noise outside. He staggered over to the window and pulled back the curtains to see a stadium filled with people. He wondered, *What kind of sports do Koreans play at four in the morning?* Frustrated, he crawled back into bed and tried to sleep through the noise coming from the stadium crowd across the street.

Later that morning he went down to the hotel lobby and asked the manager what kind of sporting event had been going on in the stadium. The hotel manager responded, "Oh, sir, that was not a sporting event. That was the church gathered for prayer."

You and I live in a culture where we gather in stadiums and around televisions for hours at a time to watch guys run around a field with a pigskin ball in their hands as they try to cross a white line. We express enthusiasm, emotion, and affection for football and other sports, and it begs the question, what would happen in our culture if the church prayed with such passion? What would happen if Jesus dominated our affections more than the superficial trivialities that garner our attention? What would happen if we spent hours before God praying on behalf of the church, the lost, and the poor around the world?

Of course, your Radical Experiment does not have to start in a stadium. It can start in your living room or prayer closet. Any-place can be the place you begin to connect the practice of prayer with the purpose of God in the world.

But back to my question: can you and I as individuals really pray specifically for the whole world? The answer is yes.

Years ago I was introduced to *Operation World,* an invaluable book by Patrick Johnstone that has revolutionized my prayer life more than any other book outside of the Bible. This book contains detailed information on every nation in the world, including sta-tistics on the religious makeup of every country, updates on gospel work in every country, and prayer requests for every country. It also includes a prayer guide that you can follow, and over the course of a year, you will pray specifically and intentionally for every nation in the world. The book has a corresponding chil-dren's version for use in families, and all the information in the book is available free online (www.operationworld.org).

Let me introduce you to Ben and Jennifer, two of the many parents in our church who use this resource to lead their families to pray boldly for the purposes of God to be accomplished in the world. They gather every evening with their two children, ages four and two, to pray specifically for different countries. Night after night their lives are being exposed to the present work of God in the world, and their hearts are being formed by the pas-sionate desire of God for the nations. In Jennifer's words, "God is opening our eyes to the specific needs of peoples around the world. It is changing our family every day and preparing us for our part in his mission."

Prayer is not flashy and probably doesn't even seem radical, but consider church history. Just a century ago the prayers of one man, Evan Roberts (1878–1951), precipitated a revival in Wales in which an estimated hundred thousand people came to faith in Christ in a matter of months. The effect reached far beyond Wales, though. A global movement began among the people of God, and ordinary Christians began scattering to the nations. In the years that followed, the Christian population in Indonesia tripled. In India, the Christian population grew sixteen times faster than the Hindu population. All around the world the nations witnessed the outpouring of God's Spirit.

Prayer can lead to effects far beyond what we can imagine. What can *your* prayer do, as it is empowered by God? Just imagine.

So the first facet of the Radical Experiment is to pray for the entire world in one year. I'm daring you to intentionally, specifically, audaciously pray for God's purpose to be accomplished around the world.

READ THROUGH THE ENTIRE WORD

The second challenge in the Radical Experiment is to read through the entire Word. And I mean just that. Systematically read through the entire Bible—Genesis 1:1 to Revelation 22:21 and all 31,101 verses in between—over the course of a year.

Our brothers and sisters around the world often gather at the risk of their lives to hear and know God's Word. If you and I are going to join them in radical obedience to Christ, we need to start with our Bibles open and our minds engaged. We have settled far too long for "Bible lite," both as individual Christians and in the community of faith. We have adopted a Christianity consumed with little devotional thoughts from God for the day, supplemented by teaching in the church filled with entertaining stories and trite opinions on how to be a better person and live a better life in the twenty-first century.

Meanwhile, we hold the matchless Word of God in our hands, and it demands a superior position in our lives, our families, our small groups, and our churches. Do we realize the battle that is waging around us? There is a true God over this world who wants all people to bow at the feet of a loving Savior, and there is a false god in this world who wants all people to burn in hell.[2] The battle is intense, and it cannot be fought with little thoughts in a daily devotional or petty ideas from a preacher on Sunday. It certainly can't be fought with minds numbed by the constant drivel of entertainment on television, DVDs, video games, and the Internet. If you and I are going to penetrate our culture and the cultures of the world with the gospel, we desperately need minds saturated with God's Word.

Now, there are many options for how this might look. A quick search on the Internet shows that Bible-reading plans abound. Some go through the Bible straight from cover to cover. Others are organized according to biblical chronology. Still others include readings from different parts of the Bible each day, and some of these are arranged thematically. Some plans involve readings every day, while other plans leave room for "catch-up days" in case you miss here or there. A plan that appeals to other people might not appeal to you. The point is simply to read the Bible. However you choose to do it—read it.

I want to put a particularly strong emphasis on this step of the Radical Experiment. The Christian marketplace is filled with books today—some of them healthy, and some of them not so healthy. To be honest, I have been very hesitant to write this book, because I look at our bookstores and think, *Do we really need another one?* I suppose only time will tell if it was worth it, but time has already spoken on one Book.

God has chosen by his matchless grace to give us revelation of himself in his Word. It is the only Book that he has promised to bless by his Spirit to transform you and me into the image of Jesus Christ. It is the only Book that he has promised to use to bring our hearts, our minds, and our lives in alignment with him. I'm not saying that God has not used or blessed other books throughout Christian history, but there is only one Book that he has perfectly inspired by his Spirit for the accomplishment of his purpose. When you or I open the Bible, we are beholding the very words of God—words that have supernatural power to redeem, renew, refresh, and restore our lives to what he created them to be.

That is why I believe it is more important for you and me to read Leviticus than it is for us to read the best Christian book ever published, because Leviticus has a quality and produces an effect that no book in the Christian marketplace can compete with. If we want to know the glory of God, if we want to experience the beauty of God, and if we want to be used by the hand of God, then we must live in the Word of God.

I realize that these first two steps in the Radical Experiment may sound anticlimactic, even disappointing, to you. What's so radical about praying and reading the Bible? My first thought is that, judging from the lack of spiritual fervency and biblical literacy in our churches today, these are extremely radical steps. But on a deeper level, think for a moment what would happen over a year as you intentionally pray for the entire world while you simultaneously read through the entire Word. After a year of such intentional praying and studying, your life cannot help but look radically different. I know this because it is the very promise of God to conform our hearts to be like his through prayer and to transform our minds to be like his through his Word.[3] In our quest for the extraordinary, we often overlook the importance of the ordinary, and I'm proposing that a radical lifestyle actually begins with an extraordinary commitment to ordinary practices that have marked Christians who have affected the world throughout history.

How will it transform your life, radicalize you, to let your mind and spirit be saturated by the Word of God day after day? This is the second component of the experiment: read the entire Bible in a year.

Sacrifice Your Money for a Specific Purpose

Notice I didn't say merely "give"; I said "sacrifice." This won't be easy, but the dividends it will pay—not just for the recipients of your sacrifice, but for you—are matchless.

You see, our hearts follow our money.[4] As we saw in chapter

6, this is a dangerous reality for American Christians and a blind spot in American Christianity. We are an affluent people living in an impoverished world. If we make only ten thousand dollars a year, we are wealthier than 84 percent of the world, and if we make fifty thousand dollars a year, we are wealthier than 99 percent of the world. Meanwhile, more than a billion people live in desperate poverty, lacking food, water, clothing, and shelter. So how can we begin to fight the battle against materialism in an effort to spend our lives—and our money—on behalf of that which is most important to the heart of God?

In our discussion of how much is enough, we briefly explored what it would look like to set a cap on our lifestyles. We thought about how we might differentiate between necessities and luxuries in order to reduce our luxuries and give away as much as possible to meet dire needs around us. We looked at John Wesley as a historical example, a man who set a cap on his lifestyle for the sake of desperate need around him. So what might this look like in your life today?

What if you took the next year and set a cap on your lifestyle? What if you sought for the next year to minimize luxuries in your life? This might involve selling present luxuries or withholding the purchase of future luxuries or intentionally sacrificing resources you already have.

I emphasize that this would be a one-year commitment for you. I point that out because there are some expenses you could postpone for one year that you might not be able to postpone for ten years. There are some things you could do without for one year that maybe you could not feasibly do without for ten years.

But what would it look like for you (or your family) to make intentional sacrifices over the next year for the glory of Christ in light of specific, urgent needs in the world?

The key word here, again, is *sacrifice*. The challenge is not just to give away excess stuff that you really don't need anyway. That's not sacrifice. Sacrifice is giving away what it hurts to give. Sacrifice is not giving according to your ability; it's giving beyond your ability.

When you begin sacrificing, the question then becomes where you are going to spend what you have sacrificed. I certainly don't want to recommend exactly where you should spend your money, but I will offer a few factors I believe are important when deciding where and how to give.

First, spend your money on something that is gospel centered. There are many organizations aimed at serving specific needs in the world, but people's greatest need in the world is Christ. To meet people's temporary physical needs apart from serving their eternal spiritual need misses the point of holistic biblical giving.

Second, and related to this, give in a way that is church focused. We will consider this in more depth in a moment, but suffice it to say here that it is not wise to bypass God's primary agent for bringing redemption to the world in an effort to meet the needs of the world. His primary agent is the church.

Third, give to a specific, tangible need. For example, if you are trying to sacrifice your money generally "to give to the poor," then you will lack a face on the need that reminds you why you must sacrifice to give. Related to this, give to someone or something you can personally serve alongside. The more you are involved with touching need personally, the more you will demonstrate the gospel to people authentically. So it's best to connect your giving to your going.

Finally, give to someone or something you can trust. We are all aware of the abuses of charitable giving in our culture, and as stewards of God's resources, we are responsible for giving to those who will handle our donation with integrity. Along these lines I also encourage you to give in sustainable ways. There are many wise and unwise ways to give to the poor. If we are not careful, we will spend our resources on short-term projects that do not have long-term effects. It is wise to spend on that which can promote long-term sustenance amid need instead of short-term satisfaction of need.

This is the third component of the Radical Experiment. For one year, sacrifice your money—every possible dollar—in order to spend your life radically on specific, urgent spiritual and physical need in the world.

SPEND YOUR TIME IN ANOTHER CONTEXT

As important as it is for us to be radical in our giving, it is even more important for us to be radical in our going. This takes us to the fourth area of the Radical Experiment. Here's where it gets personal. Here's where your heart is going to be touched, possibly in a way that it never has before.

I don't know if you have ever gone anywhere away from home, whether a car ride away or a plane ride away, to share the gospel or care for the needy in Christ's name. But whether you have or you haven't, you need to do this in the coming year to fully enter into the agenda God has for your life. I know some people raise objections, but they fall down in the face of reality.

I remember when I was first preparing to go to Sudan, a nation impoverished by years of civil war. The trip was going to cost me around three thousand dollars. It wasn't easy to travel into Sudan since they were still at war, and we would have to charter a plane and spend a few extra days to make that happen. I remember one dear lady in the church coming up to me and asking, "Why don't you just send the three thousand dollars to the people in Sudan? Wouldn't that be a better use of money than your spending a week and a half with them? Think of how far that money could go."

I wrestled with that question. Was I wasting these funds in order to go when I could simply give the money instead? Should I even be going? I continued wrestling with that question until I got to Sudan. There I had a conversation with Andrew that shed some light on the question.

Andrew was sharing with me about his life in Sudan over the last twenty years. He had known war since he was born, and he described facets of the suffering and persecution his people had been through. He told me about the various groups, most of them secular or government organizations, who had brought supplies to them during that time, and he expressed thanks for the generosity of so many people.

But then he looked at me and asked, "Even in light of all these things that people have given us, do you want to know how you can tell who a true brother is?"

I leaned forward and asked, "How?"

He responded, "A true brother comes to be with you in your time of need." Then he looked me in the eye and said, "David, you are a true brother. Thank you for coming to be with us."

Tears welled up in my eyes as the reality of the gospel hit home with me in an entirely new way. I was immediately reminded that when God chose to bring salvation to you and me, he did not send gold or silver, cash or check. He sent himself—the Son. I was convicted for even considering that I should give money instead of actually coming to Sudan. How will I ever show the gospel to the world if all I send is my money? Was I really so shallow as to think that my money is the answer to the needs in the world?

If we are going to accomplish the global purpose of God, it will not be primarily through giving our money, as important as that is. It will happen primarily through giving ourselves. This is what the gospel represents, and it's what the gospel requires.

So how will we go? For each one of us, this clearly begins at home. Wherever you and I live, we are commanded to go and make disciples there. In light of Jesus' example, our primary impact on the nations will occur in the disciple making we do right around us. Remember that Jesus didn't travel to every place in the world while he was on earth, and he didn't go to all the multitudes. He poured his life into a few men for the sake of the multitudes in places he would never go. Therefore, our homes, communities, and cities are the primary places and contain the primary people with whom we will impact nations for the glory of Christ.

Over the last few years, our church has experienced a subtle yet significant shift in how we understand "going." For a time we were trying to organize and centralize all the various types of community ministries we were involved in. The problem, however, was that the more we encouraged and equipped people to go and make disciples of all nations, the harder it was to try to control all that they were doing. That's when we sat back and realized that the last thing we needed to do was to control everything that everyone was doing! So we decentralized all these ministries and instead focused on empowering men and women to start, manage, and lead ministries all across our city.

The effect was subtly amazing. Every one of our small groups began looking at the gifts, skills, and passions represented in their group and then prayed about how God wanted to use them to multiply the gospel by making disciples in the community around them. Instead of organizing a Vacation Bible School on our campus, small groups across our city started leading week-long Bible clubs in their homes. They found that they could share the gospel with their neighbors far more effectively by simply inviting them to their houses. This poured over into igniting other types of ministries. Every week now our faith family is leading Bible studies in workplaces and neighborhoods, helping addicts in rehabilitation centers, serving food in homeless shelters, teaching orphans in learning centers, caring for widows in retirement homes, providing hospice care for the elderly, training men and women in job skills, tutoring men and women in reading, rocking sick babies in hospitals, helping patients in AIDS clinics, teaching English to internationals, and doing a variety of other things, all in an effort to multiply the gospel—and we haven't had to organize any of it!

The possibilities are limitless when the people of God are equipped and empowered to accomplish the purpose of God in the context of where they live day in and day out.

Going starts where we live, but it doesn't stop there, and this is where we come to the fourth component of the Radical Experiment. If there are a billion people who have never heard the gospel and billions of others who still have not received the gospel, then we have an obligation to go to them. This is not an option. This is a command, not a calling. What is a matter of calling is where we will go and how long we will stay. We will not all go to the same places, and we will not all stay the same length of time. But it is clearly the will of God for us to take the gospel to the nations.

So, the fourth challenge in the Radical Experiment is to give some of your time in the next year to making the gospel known in a context outside your own city. I suggest you plan on dedicating at least 2 percent of your time to this task. That 2 percent works out to be about one week in the next year that you will travel and take the gospel to another context in the world, either domestically or internationally.

At the end of every year, men and women across our church embrace this particular challenge, and the result is literally week-to-week stories of where they have gone and what they have seen God do. We have discovered that 2 percent of our time living out the gospel in other contexts has a radical effect on the other 98 percent of our time living out the gospel in our own context.

Almost every Sunday someone or some group will come up

to me and tell me about what they have experienced sharing the gospel in another context that week. One particular Sunday an entire group of people approached me with smiles on their faces. They had just returned from Latin America. Most of them did not even know one another a week prior, but now they were locked arm in arm, overflowing with excitement about all they had seen God do.

This group decided that if they could go all the way to another country together to share the gospel, they could do the same in our community. So they started meeting every week and then going periodically into a housing project in the inner city, where they would host cookouts and carnivals. It didn't take long for them to realize, though, that if they really wanted to make disciples in the inner city, they would need to do more than just go down there every once in a while. As a result, they decided to move their small group meeting to the housing project, where they began gathering with people there to study the Bible together every week. In the days that followed, they started various ministries for children in the area and saw numerous men and women come to faith in Christ from drug- and violence-ridden backgrounds. Multiplication of the gospel in Latin America led to multiplication of the gospel in inner-city Birmingham, Alabama. Not either-or, but both-and!

The story does not end there, though. The fruit of that small group's ministry now extends to an organization that some of the men created to provide underprivileged teenagers with the opportunity to go to college and grow in Christ in order to be prepared to, in their words, "go into all the world multiplying the gospel by making disciples." Another family has brought an otherwise homeless man into their home to help him get back on his feet.

Simply put, the multiplication effect of making disciples in all nations does not end. When a group of people decided to give 2 percent of their lives to making the gospel known in another context around the world, they had no idea how radically it would transform the other 98 percent of their lives in their own context.

I am convinced that when we open up our lives to the global purpose of God, he will show us things we have never seen and take us places we have never been before. We will realize that God has given us gifts, skills, and passions that he desires to use in unique ways around the world. I think of Adam, who excels in his work with a wheelchair company in Alabama but who also goes to Romania to help fit impoverished and handicapped men and women there with wheelchairs. I think of Darryl, who works construction here and then goes to Ecuador to help build homes for families that have nothing. I think of Will, who is a veterinarian here yet also travels to a struggling reservation in Arizona to help them with their cattle.

I think of Andrea. She is a college student who, by her own admission, doesn't like college. Upon graduation from high school, she immediately wanted to go to another country. In her words, "I did not want to go to college because I felt like it would be a waste of time. After all, people were dying without Christ, and I did not have time to be educated." Her parents wisely persuaded her to go to school in Alabama, far away from Asia or Africa, where she really wanted to be.

Andrea struggled with the relevance of school until one day in our worship gathering we were talking about the needs among the Bedouin people, most of whom had never heard the gospel, and it clicked. Andrea was in school for the sake of the Bedouin. As soon as she was able, she signed up for Arabic classes. Not long after beginning these classes, she e-mailed me that she was going to spend a semester studying Arabic in the Middle East, where she would have the opportunity to be among the Bedouin people. She wrote, "I wanted to let you know that Brook Hills is going to run into the Bedouin people this semester, and I will have the opportunity to tell them about Jesus."

Consider what happens when all of us begin to look at our professions and areas of expertise not merely as means to an income or to career paths in our own context but as platforms for proclaiming the gospel in contexts around the world. Consider what happens when the church is not only sending traditional missionaries around the world but also businessmen and businesswomen, teachers and students, doctors and politicians, engineers and technicians who are living out the gospel in contexts where a traditional missionary could never go.

If we are not careful, this 2 percent commitment may even lead us one day to give 98 percent of our time in another context so that we come back to our American context for a 2 percent visit each year. The point is not where we go, how we get there, or even how long we stay. The point is simply that we go.

So where will you go? How will you let God stretch you? The challenge is, as an individual or as a family, to spend 2 percent of your time over the next year going to another context in the world with the gospel.

COMMIT YOUR LIFE TO A
MULTIPLYING COMMUNITY

The final component of the Radical Experiment is to commit your life to a multiplying community. I save this challenge for last because it is where the other four challenges converge. As we explored in chapter 5, Christ's command to make disciples is an invitation to give our lives for the sake of others. God has created us for community with one another, and the community we were created for is called the church. As part of a vibrant community of faith, you will have support and encouragement to live out your intention to be radically abandoned to Jesus.

It is a glorious privilege to be a part of the universal body of Christ, united with brothers and sisters across the world and across history in a heavenly community. But it is also the New Testament pattern for us to be a part of a local body of Christ, a gathering of brothers and sisters in a particular location where our Christianity comes to life in commitment to one another. By the design of God, the local church affects every facet of our Christian lives.

We pray for the entire world, but we do not pray alone. We pray, "*Our* Father in heaven…" Our praying is integrally connected to the wider community of faith of which we are a part. We read through the entire Word, but we need one another to under-stand it, to learn it, and to apply it. We sacrifice our money for a specific purpose, and we spend our time in another context, but we are not lone rangers trying to accomplish the purpose of God. Our giving and our going must be tied to the multiplication of the gospel through the church.

Therefore, if you are not a committed, active, devoted mem-ber of a local church, then fundamentally the Radical Experiment involves committing your life to a community of faith. Through-out the book we have seen how radical obedience to Christ affects the way we operate as local churches. This was not intended simply to be pastor-speak. The goal is not just for us as individuals to fol-low after Christ but to join together in communities of faith, denying ourselves, taking up our crosses, and following after him.

After the rich young man of Mark 10 left with his possessions, Jesus looked at his disciples and told them that some of them would lose their families because they followed him. But then he told them that they would receive more than they ever had before in brothers, sisters, and mothers, all together under their heavenly Father. This is an amazing family portrait and a remarkable reminder of the beauty of New Testament community.

The reality is, we need community in order to follow Christ radically. I am convinced that one reason many of us have not taken radical steps in our giving, for example, may not be so much because we love our possessions as it is because we fear isolation. If the radical, simple living we see Jesus talking about were more common in the church, it would be much easier for us to live sim-ply as well. But we look around, and everyone else has nice cars, nice homes, and lifestyles characterized by luxuries, so we accept that this must be the norm for Christians. We may get convicted about our way of living when we look at the Bible, but then when we look at one another, we assume it must be okay because everyone else lives this way.

If we are going to live in radical obedience to Christ, we will need the church to do it. We will need to show one another how to give liberally, go urgently, and live dangerously. When we sacrifice our resources for the poor and then face unexpected and unforeseen needs in our own lives, we will need brothers and sisters to help us stand. In the process we will learn to depend on one another according to God's design. The global purpose of Christ was never intended to be accomplished by individuals. We are a global people whose family spans the nations. So first and foremost, I encourage you to be done with church hopping and shopping in a me-centered cultural milieu and to commit your life to a people who need you and whom you need.

Then once you commit your life to a local church, or if you are already committed to a local church, look for the best avenue within that community of faith to be about making disciples. In the church I pastor, this happens primarily through small groups— men and women committed to sharing the Word with the lost, showing and teaching the Word to one another, and serving the world together. Jesus placed a fundamental priority on disciplemaking relationships, and such relationships cannot play a merely supplemental part in our Christian lives.

So who are the band of disciples that you are going to join with for the next year in this Radical Experiment? Alongside whom will you go into the community and into other contexts? With whom will you share the life of Christ as you show them what it means to follow after him? To whom will you teach the Word as God teaches you over the next year? How are you going to intentionally make disciples?

We cannot overestimate the effect of believers who begin living out the claims of the gospel together in churches. I received the following "critical" letter recently from a man in our church. I have included it here in its entirety to illustrate what happens when people who do not know Christ see the gospel at work in the church. This man wrote:

Dear Dr. Platt and the Church at Brook Hills,

I assume, based upon what others have said about you and the faith family at Brook Hills, that you are accustomed to receiving complimentary letters. I hope that you will indulge me as I write to you from a different perspective. My letter could be considered more of a complaint or a warning. It is intended to enlighten you as to how your "radical" actions and teachings related to the Word have been destroying my life and probably the lives of others like me.

Let me explain... I was raised, unchurched, by loving parents who were perfectly content with their lives. The worldly perspective I grew up with allowed me to see the hypocrisy in the lives of the few churchgoing families to which I had been exposed. Thus as I grew into a worldly man, I found myself on the path to the American dream. This path, as far as I could see, did not go through or even near a church. I went to college and then grad school, married a kind and beautiful woman, and got a decent, respectable job, which allowed me to ultimately buy a house or at least make payments on a mortgage and make maximum contributions to a 401(k). My wife and I eventually had a family with two beautiful daughters and a couple of dogs. I was living the middle class version of the American dream.

I was a kind, decent family man who was grounded in the realities of the world. I was perfectly content to devote myself to working hard to provide the financial resources my family would need: 401(k) retirement plan, 529 college savings plan, a general savings account, and a vacation savings account. I also worked to provide the necessities of life such as a flat screen TV. My charitable giving could be described as minimal at best. I loved my family and loved spending time with them, but I was constantly distracted by the financial realities and needs of our lives. I looked to my balance statements for a sense of security.

Like many good, worldly men devoted to getting ahead in this world, I would find moments of joy when the quarterly 401(k) statement showed a profit. I also experienced pronounced periods of stress, disappointment, and anger when the 401(k) dropped or when we had to take money out of savings to pay the bills. However, I accepted these ups and downs as the realities of life, and overall we were doing okay.

Then one day my wife, who I thought loved me, told me that she would like to raise our daughters in a church and requested that we start visiting local churches. Up to this point in my life, I had done a good job of avoiding churches and the hypocritical Christians who attended them. I had always felt uncomfortable around faith-professing Christians because I lacked biblical knowledge and assumed they would look down on me. Now, in order to make my wife happy, I was going to have to attend a church and interact with those people on their turf. I reluctantly agreed and added church to my list of dreaded weekend chores. Initially our trial run at visiting churches proved relatively painless. The people were nice, but the watered-down version of the Word they were serving had little impact and left me with no desire for more. My wife, who was also unimpressed by these experiences, suggested we try Brook Hills because she had heard good things about this church. Well, if attending a regular church was bad, I was sure attending a megachurch would be worse. However, as usual, my wife convinced me, and we attended your church for the first time last fall. That day was the start of a process in which you and your faith family have been progressively destroying my life in this world.

The Word you served up that day was strong and pure, not like the watered-down versions I had received in the past. It had an immediate impact on me and, like the most addictive drugs, left me wanting more. We started to attend fairly regularly on Sundays, but soon that was not enough to satisfy my growing need for more of this Word. I started buying CDs of previous sermons so I could get my fix on the way to and from work each day. I started to interact more with members of this faith family who were not only consuming the Word but also appeared to be living it as well. This only fueled my desire for more. Soon we were attending a small group on Sundays in addition to the service and were occasionally attending a Wednesday night Bible study.

You and this faith family seemed all too happy to encourage and support my habit. As I got deeper and deeper into this addiction, a side effect known as faith began to grow inside of me. As my faith grew, I felt a greater need for fellowship with others suffering with this same faith. All along I was gradually losing my grip on the realities of this world, which had been my foundation, and I came to Christ.

I cannot believe what the Word and this growing faith have done to my life over the past year. I used to avoid church altogether. Now we attend the worship services on Sundays and have joined a small group, which meets for three to five hours each week at a neighbor's house. I attend a class on how to study the Bible. I used to avoid Christians who professed their faith, and now I am becoming one. I find myself seeking opportunities to share the Word and discuss my growing faith with others.

I stopped saving for the flat screen TV, which is just as well since I don't have much time for TV anymore. I have reduced my 401(k) contributions and stopped looking at the quarterly statements. I have gone from trying to save as much money as I could to trying to find ways to give some of our savings away in addition to regular contributions to the church and various faith-based charities devoted to the poor and other ministries. Strangely enough this brings me greater joy than I ever experienced with a quarterly 401(k) statement showing a profit.

What is wrong with me? It's lunacy!!! What have you done to me?

The worldly man I was a year ago would not recognize the man I am becoming. I was a man believing in the realities of this world, living the American dream, saving up riches for a comfortable future, and looking for security in a strong bottom line. Now I believe in, pray to, and seek after a relationship with a God I cannot see. I have found salvation in Christ, whom I cannot see. I long for eternity in an unseen future creation. I now look for security in my faith. All of this would have sounded like foolishness to the man I was a year ago. However, the man I was a year ago and the worldly life I knew are being destroyed. This has obviously had an impact on me, but it has also impacted my family, whom I pray with daily.

I wanted you and the faith family at Brook Hills to be aware of the role you have played in destroying my worldly life. I also feel the need to warn you that if you persist in teaching and living out the Word as you are doing currently, then you will likely have a similar impact on the worldly lives of others like me. I hope you realize that you may have to live with the knowledge of your actions and their effect on the lives of others for all of eternity. I will be there in eternity to remind you of what you have done.

Sincerely,
Your brother in Christ

I praise God for what happens when the church comes together to display a radical gospel. Indeed, the church is God's plan for multiplying the gospel to all nations, and where Christians lock arms with one another in communities of faith pursuing a radical Savior, the very gates of hell cannot stop the spread of God's glory. So this is the final step in the Radical Experiment: commit your life to a community of believers that is intentionally multiplying the gospel by making disciples.

A DREAM

This is the Radical Experiment. Over the next year to pray for the entire world. To read through the entire Word. To sacrifice your money for a specific purpose. To spend your time in another context. To commit your life to a multiplying community. Will you take the challenge? In light of all that we have seen, will you take these practical steps to break out of the American dream and to begin abandoning your life to a radical gospel?

Consider what you might feel after a year of being intimately exposed to the heart of God for every nation in the world. Contemplate what you might know about the glory of God after a year of listening closely to his voice. Think of all the possessions you have now that you would realize you do not need, and think of all the dire needs that would be met as a result of your sacrifice of them. Wonder about where God might lead you—near or far, to a reached people or maybe to an unreached people who have never heard the gospel until they meet you. Reflect on the community of faith that would surround you as you find yourself in relationships that are the primary avenue through which your life will impact the world.

What happens when men and women begin following Christ with all their hearts into all the world? In this book I have sought to crack open the door and provide a glimpse into what it might look like. But this book is just that: a glimpse.

I want to help you in this. And I want to connect you with resources and people who, like you, are on a journey of radically following Jesus. Go to the Web site that accompanies this book (www.radicalthebook.com) for more stories, links, and helps that can make your one-year experiment a thrilling success. And please, if God is doing something special in your life as a result of your Radical Experiment, leave a story about it on the Web site so that others can be encouraged.

I have so much more to uncover about radical discipleship to Jesus, and the church I am a part of has so much more to explore.

I fear that in sharing some of their stories, I have communicated that everything in our church is aligned with the person and purpose of Christ. Unfortunately it is not. We have far to go. I also fear that I have given the impression that everything goes smoothly and wonderfully when we attempt to recover the essence of the gospel in the church. Let me assure you that the opposite is true. I have wondered if it might be beneficial to include an additional chapter filled with the not-so-positive e-mails that have come my way as we have tried to work out the core truths of the gospel in our faith family! I am not without fault, and I have made many mistakes. I have so much to learn about what it means to be a pastor, and the great evidence of God's grace is that the church I pastor has stuck with me as long as they have. I love them more than I could have imagined when I first started to lead them, and one of the deepest, most undeserved joys of my life is pastoring a church in America that I believe, under the power of the Holy Spirit of God, can shake the nations for his glory.

I also fear that in addressing unbiblical foundations inherent within the American dream, I have created the impression that every facet of the American dream is negative. This is certainly not the case. Though we have much to learn from our persecuted brothers and sisters in lands where there is no freedom, and though we have much to learn from impoverished brothers and sisters in lands where there are few resources, I am grateful to God for the freedom and resources he has given us in the United States. These gifts from God have certainly not been without cost, and if we did not have such freedoms and resources, many of the opportunities we have to take the gospel to the nations would simply not exist.

The challenge before us, then, is to use the freedoms, resources, and opportunities God has entrusted to us for his purpose in the world, all the while remaining careful not to embrace ideas, values, and assumptions that contradict what God has said in his Word.

We have seen the cost of following Jesus. Give up everything you have. Sell your possessions, and give to the poor. Go to places of great need and great danger, where you may lose your life. Give your life for the sake of Christ among the nations. The cost of picking up a cross and following Jesus is steep. It costs you everything you have. But in the end, the reward is sweet. You gain more than you ever had.

In the words of Jesus, "No one who has left home or brothers or sisters or mother or father or children or fields for me and the gospel will fail to receive a hundred times as much in this present age…and in the age to come, eternal life."[5] When you do the math on this, this really is no sacrifice. In the introduction to Jim Elliot's biography, his wife, Elisabeth, wrote a summary of his life and death that seems most appropriate at this point. She said:

> Jim's aim was to know God. His course, obedience—the only course that could lead to the fulfillment of his aim. His end was what some would call an extraordinary death, although in facing death he had quietly pointed out that many have died because of obedience to God.
>
> He and the other men with whom he died were hailed as heroes, "martyrs." I do not approve. Nor would they have approved.
>
> Is the distinction between living for Christ and dying

for Him, after all, so great? Is not the second the logical conclusion of the first? Furthermore, to live for God *is* to die, "daily," as the apostle Paul put it. It is to lose everything that we may gain Christ. It is in thus laying down our lives that we find them.[6]

As Elisabeth Elliot points out, not even dying a martyr's death is classified as extraordinary obedience when you are following a Savior who died on a cross. Suddenly a martyr's death seems like normal obedience.

So what happens when radical obedience to Christ becomes the new normal? Are you willing to see? You have a choice. You can cling to short-term treasures that you cannot keep, or you can live for long-term treasures that you cannot lose: people coming to Christ; men, women, and children living because they now have food; unreached tribes receiving the gospel. And the all-consuming satisfaction of knowing and experiencing Christ as the treasure above all others.

You and I have an average of about seventy or eighty years on this earth. During these years we are bombarded with the temporary. Make money. Get stuff. Be comfortable. Live well. Have fun. In the middle of it all, we get blinded to the eternal. But it's there. You and I stand on the porch of eternity. Both of us will soon stand before God to give an account for our stewardship of the time, the resources, the gifts, and ultimately the gospel he has entrusted to us. When that day comes, I am convinced we will not wish we had given more of ourselves to living the American dream. We will not wish we had made more money, acquired more stuff, lived more comfortably, taken more vacations, watched more television, pursued greater retirement, or been more successful in the eyes of this world. Instead we will wish we had given more of ourselves to living for the day when every nation, tribe, people, and language will bow around the throne and sing the praises of the Savior who delights in radical obedience and the God who deserves eternal worship.

Are you ready to live for this dream? Let's not waver any longer.

MY RADICAL EXPERIMENT

I agree with the *Radical* claim that I can find satisfaction and real service to God only in abandonment to Jesus. So I hereby commit to a one-year experiment of radical living according to the gospel...and to making myself open to the permanent changes God wants to perform in my life as a result of this experiment.

Over the next year...

1. I will pray for the entire world.

   To make this commitment real in my life, I choose here and now specifically to _____

   _____

   _____ .

2. I will read through the entire Word.

   To make this commitment real in my life, I choose here and now specifically to _____

   _____

   _____ .

3. I will sacrifice my money for a specific purpose.

   To make this commitment real in my life, I choose
   here and now specifically to _____

   _____

   _____ .

4. I will spend time in another context.

   To make this commitment real in my life, I choose
   here and now specifically to _____

   _____

   _____ .

5. I will commit my life to a multiplying community.

   To make this commitment real in my life, I choose
   here and now specifically to _____

   _____

   _____ .

Signed _____

Date _____

ACKNOWLEDGMENTS

This work is the fruit of God's grace expressed to me in innumerable ways.

I am indebted to Randy, Sealy, and Jeana for believing in this book; Ken and the folks at Multnomah for taking it on; Dave for bringing it to fruition; and Mark for keeping it true. I do not deserve the kindness you all have shown me.

I am indebted to Dad, Eddie, Gregg, Franklin, and Jim for investing your lives in mine. I pray that in eternity my life will prove worthy of all you have poured into me.

I am indebted to the elders, staff, and members of the Church at Brook Hills for giving me the privilege of being your pastor. In the words of Paul, I love and long for you, my joy and my crown (Philippians 4:1).

I am indebted to my family for constantly loving me and patiently supporting me. Mom, thank you for all the sacrifices you make for your children and grandchildren. Heather, Caleb, Joshua, and the precious child we are in the process of adopting, please know that the great honor of my life is being your husband and dad.

May God's grace to me be to great effect for him (John 3:30).

Notes

Chapter 1: Someone Worth Losing Everything For

1. John 6:53
2. John 6:66–67
3. Luke 9:57–58
4. Luke 9:60
5. Luke 9:62
6. Luke 14:26
7. Luke 14:27
8. Luke 14:33
9. Mark 10:17
10. Mark 10:21
11. Dietrich Bonhoeffer, *The Cost of Discipleship* (New York: Simon and Schuster, 1995), 89.
12. Mark 10:21
13. Matthew 13:44

Chapter 2: Too Hungry for Words

1. Sovereign Creator: Nehemiah 9:6; Psalm 24:1–2. Knows all things: Job 37:16; 1 John 3:20. Sustains all things: Psalms 36:6; 104:24–30. Owns all things: Deuteronomy 10:14. Holy: 1 Samuel 2:2. Righteous: Deuteronomy 32:4. Just in wrath: Romans 3:5–6. Loving: 1 John 4:16.
2. Habakkuk 1:13
3. Psalm 5:5
4. John 3:16, 36

5. John 8:34; 2 Timothy 2:26

6. Romans 5:10–12; 6:23; 8:10; Ephesians 2:1, 3; 5:14; James 4:4

7. Matthew 26:39; see also Psalm 75:8; Isaiah 51:22; Jeremiah 25:15; Revelation 14:10

8. Even John's words about receiving Jesus (John 1:12–13) are misconstrued in our day to communicate a more casual approval of Christ instead of a wholehearted trust in Christ.

9. Matthew 7:21–23

10. Ephesians 2:8–9

Chapter 3: Beginning at the End of Ourselves

1. James Truslow Adams, *The Epic of America* (Boston: Little, Brown, 1933), 415.

2. John 15:5

3. 2 Corinthians 12:7–9

4. Joshua 6:3–5

5. Acts 1:14

6. Acts 4:13

7. Acts 5:12

8. George Muller, *Answers to Prayer,* comp. A. E. C. Brooks (Chicago: Moody, n.d.), 9–10, emphasis added.

9. Luke 11:11–13

10. Matthew 7:11

11. John 14:15–19, KJV

12. John 16:13

13. Spirit of wisdom: Ephesians 1:17. Spirit of power: Acts 1:8; 2 Timothy 1:7. Fruit of the Spirit: Galatians 5:22–23.

14. John 14:12–14

Chapter 4: The Great Why of God

1. Genesis 1:26–27
2. Genesis 1:28
3. Genesis 12:2–3
4. Exodus 14:4
5. Daniel 3:28–29
6. Psalms 23:3; 67; Isaiah 43:1–13
7. Ezekiel 36:22–23
8. Matthew 28:18–20; Mark 16:15; Luke 24:47–49; also Acts 1:8
9. Revelation 7:9–10

Chapter 5: The Multiplying Community

1. John 17:4
2. John 17:6, 10, 12, 13, 19
3. Matthew 28:18–20
4. Romans 6:1–4
5. 1 Corinthians 12:12–13; Ephesians 4:4–6

Chapter 6: How Much Is Enough?

1. Proverbs 28:27; Isaiah 3:13–26; Jeremiah 5:26–29; Amos 2:6–7; 4:1–3; 8:3–10; Luke 6:24–26; James 5:1–6
2. Matthew 25:41
3. This particularly applies to our needy brothers and sisters in Christ. This is the emphasis of Christ in Matthew 25:31–36; the picture of the church in Acts 2:42–47 and 4:32–37; and the intent of Paul, James, and John in 2 Corinthians 8–9, James 2, and 1 John 3, respectively.
4. See especially James 2:14–26; 1 John 3:11–24.

5. Clearly, there are many differences between sexual sin and material sin. The point here is simply that we are tempted to sin in both our sexual lives and our material lives, and in both cases we need to repent. Regarding neglect as sin, see particularly James 4:17.

6. 1 Timothy 6:17

7. 2 Corinthians 8:9

8. Luke 16:25–26

9. Hears: Job 34:28. Feeds: Psalm 68:10. Satisfies: Psalm 22:26. Rescues: Psalm 35:10. Defends: Psalm 82:3. Raises up: 1 Samuel 2:8; Psalm 113:7. Secures justice: Psalm 140:12.

10. The rich man's lack of faith in God is further evidenced at the end of this story, where Jesus asserts that the Pharisees had rejected both the Son of God and the Word of God.

11. Again, I want to be very cautious here not to imply that caring for the poor is the grounds or basis of our salvation. As we saw in the second chapter, the work of Christ on the cross is the basis of our salvation, and faith in him is the means by which God saves us. One fruit of our faith is concern for the poor (see James 2:14–19 and 1 John 3:16–18). So the people of God, when they study the truth of God's Word and see the need around them in the world, will subsequently respond with the compassion of Christ.

12. Mark 10:23–24

13. Genesis 20:14–16; 26:12–15; 30:43; 47:27; Leviticus 26:3–5, 9–13; Deuteronomy 28:1–14

14. 1 Kings 8:56–66

15. Mark 10:21–26

16. For an in-depth discussion of this assertion, see Craig L. Blomberg, *Neither Poverty nor Riches: A Biblical Theology of Material Possessions,* ed. D. A. Carson (Downers Grove, IL: InterVarsity, 1999). Blomberg writes, "The New Testament carried forward the major principles of the Old Testament and intertestamental Judaism with one conspicuous omission: never was material wealth promised as a guaranteed reward for either spiritual obedience or simple hard work." He continues, "Material reward for piety never reappears in Jesus' teaching, and is explicitly contradicted throughout" (pages 242, 145).

17. 1 Corinthians 6:19

18. Mark 10:17, 21

19. Jesus teaches us that this kind of faith is possible only by the grace of God (Mark 10:27).

20. In Luke 12:33, Jesus reiterates the same command: "Sell your possessions and give to the poor."

21. Robert H. Gundry, *Matthew: A Commentary on His Handbook for a Mixed Church under Persecution,* 2nd ed. (Grand Rapids: Eerdmans, 1994), 388.

22. Luke 14:33

23. Mark 10:17

24. Luke 12:32–33

25. 1 Timothy 6:9

26. Charles Edward White, "Four Lessons on Money from One of the World's Richest Preachers," *Christian History* 7, no. 19 (1998): 24.

27. 2 Corinthians 8:14; 9:11

28. 2 Corinthians 8:14

29. John Calvin, *Commentary on the Epistles of Paul the Apostle to the Corinthians,* trans. John Pringle (Grand Rapids: Baker Book, 2003), 1:297.

30. John Calvin, *Calvin: Institutes of the Christian Religion,* ed., John T. McNeill, trans. Ford Lewis Battles (Philadelphia: Westminster Press, 1960), 2:1098.

31. Calvin, *Commentary on the Epistles,* 1:297.

32. 1 Timothy 6:18

33. 2 Corinthians 8:2

34. Mark 10:28

35. James 1:27

36. Proverbs 6:6–8; 21:20; Luke 12:16–21; James 5:1–6

37. Mark 10:22

38. Matthew 6:21

Chapter 7: There Is No Plan B

1. Interestingly, Paul wrote the book of Romans to convince the Christians in that city to help him take the gospel to people who had never heard. Specifically, he wanted to go to Spain (Romans 15:24). His ambition was to "preach the gospel where Christ was not known" (verse 20), and the people of Spain had never heard of Christ. Moreover, I am indebted to R. C. Sproul for his brief excerpt on the destiny of the unevangelized in his *Reason to Believe: A Response to Common Objections to Christianity* (Grand Rapids: Zondervan, 1982), 58–59. The thoughts I share here are the development of various truths he proposes there.

2. Romans 1:19–20

3. Romans 1:21

4. Romans 1:21

5. Romans 1:21–25

6. Romans 1:25

7. Romans 1:24, 26, 29–32

8. Romans 3:10–12

9. Romans 3:19

10. Romans 3:20

11. This is the case Paul builds when comparing Jews and Gentiles in Romans 2:12–16.

12. Romans 3:21–22

13. Romans 5:1

14. Romans 10:9–10

15. Romans 10:13–15

16. Acts 10

Chapter 8: Living When Dying Is Gain

1. Matthew 10:39

2. Matthew 10:8

3. Matthew 10:16

4. Matthew 10:21

5. Matthew 10:22

6. Matthew 10:23

7. 2 Timothy 3:12

8. Matthew 10:24–25

9. Luke 6:40

10. Philippians 1:29

11. Matthew 10:26, 28, 31

12. Matthew 10:29

13. Colossians 1:24

14. Acts 8:1, 4

15. Matthew 10:30–31

16. Matthew 10:28

17. Philippians 1:21

18. Revelation 12:11

19. John G. Paton, *John G. Paton, D.D., Missionary to the New Hebrides: An Autobiography* (London: Hodder and Stoughton, 1891), 56.

20. Elisabeth Elliot, *Shadow of the Almighty: The Life and Testament of Jim Elliot* (San Francisco: HarperCollins, 1979), 132.

21. Norman Grubb, *C. T. Studd: Cricketer and Pioneer* (Fort Washington, PA: CLC Publications, 2001), 120–21.

22. Hebrews 11:16

23. Erich Bridges, "Worldview: Remembering a Young Woman Who Followed God to the Desert," *Baptist Press*, August 1, 2002, www.bpnews.net/printerfriendly.asp?ID=13951.

Chapter 9: The Radical Experiment

1. Matthew 9:36–38

2. 2 Corinthians 4:4–6

3. Matthew 6:9–15; 2 Timothy 3:16–17

4. Matthew 6:19–21

5. Mark 10:29–30

6. Elisabeth Elliot, *Shadow of the Almighty: The Life and Testament of Jim Elliot* (San Francisco: HarperCollins, 1979), 9–10.

About the Author

DR. DAVID PLATT is the lead pastor of the Church at Brook Hills, a four-thousand-member congregation in Birmingham, Alabama, that describes itself as "a faith family full of world-impacting disciples who really believe that as a church we can shake the nations for God's glory."

David's first love in ministry is disciple making—teaching God's Word, mentoring others, and multiplying the gospel. "I believe that God has uniquely created every one of his people to impact the world," he says. "God is in the business of blessing his people so that his ways and his salvation might be made known among all people." To this end, David has traveled throughout the United States and around the world teaching the Bible and training church leaders.

David has earned two undergraduate degrees from the University of Georgia and three advanced degrees, including a doctor of philosophy from New Orleans Baptist Theological Seminary. Prior to coming to Brook Hills, he served the seminary as dean of chapel and assistant professor of expository preaching and apologetics and was on staff at Edgewater Baptist Church in New Orleans. He is the founder of Radical, a nonprofit organization providing multilingual resources, events, and other avenues to support disciple making through the local church. David and his wife, Heather, are Atlanta natives. They currently live with their family in Birmingham.

To learn more about the Radical Experiment,
go to radicalexperiment.org.

To learn more about Radical, the ministry, visit Radical.net.

ADDITIONAL RESOURCES

Available as a 10-pack, ideal for church giveaways, welcome packets, or small group distribution

In *Radical Together,* David Platt follows up his revolutionary call to authentic discipleship with the next big step: showing how it can work in your church.

Find information, tools for individual application, church resources, and videos at Radicalthebook.com

---

ALSO AVAILABLE

This resource will help you discover what could happen if the message of *Radical* and *Radical Together* were lived out by every member of your church.

Small-Group study available from Lifeway.

David Platt issues a wake-up call to the church, compelling us to examine the validity of our own personal faith. There's a cost to *truly* giving yourself to Christ's call: "Follow me." **Are you truly a follower of Christ?**